Baby
blueprint
crochet

irresistible projects
for little ones

robyn
chachula

INTERWEAVE
interweave.com

Editor Katrina Loving
Technical Editor Karen Manthey
Designer Marissa Bowers
Photographer Joe Coca
Production Katherine Jackson

Interweave Press LLC
201 East Fourth Street
Loveland, CO 80537
interweave.com

Printed in China by Asia Pacific Offset Ltd.

Library of Congress
Cataloging-in-Publication Data

Chachula, Robyn, 1978-
Baby blueprint crochet :
irresistible projects for little ones /
Robyn Chachula.
p. cm.
  Includes bibliographical references and index.
  ISBN 978-1-59668-201-6 (pbk.)
  1. Crocheting--Patterns.
  2. Crocheting--Designs.
  3. Infants' clothing. I. Title.
  TT825.C3775 2010
  746.43'4--dc22
2010013192

10 9 8 7 6 5 4 3 2 1

Dedication

This book is dedicated to my muse, Elianna, my four-month-old daughter, who was with me every step of the way, from sketching to design. Thank you for being my best creation yet.

Acknowledgments

I had numerous talented and crafty crocheters help me make a number of the samples for the book. They are Rebecca DeSensi, Virginia Boundy, Chie O'Briant, Diane Halpern, and Megan Granholm. Without their help I would not have slept for six months, so bless you for all your wonderful work.

The yarns used in the book were all donated graciously by the yarn companies. They are Blue Sky Alpacas, Classic Elite Yarns, Tahki Stacy Charles, Lion Brand, Caron International, and Coats and Clark. Thank you so much for all your support and quick response to all my requests; I truly appreciate all that you have given me.

Thank you to everyone at Interweave, especially Katrina Loving and Karen Manthey, for making the ramblings of a sleep-deprived new mom sound intelligent.

Most importantly, I would like to thank my friends and family for all their love and support in every crazy challenge I take on. I would especially like to thank my husband, Mark, for his unwavering love. Without his encouragement and help, this book would not have been possible.

Lastly, I want to thank you, the reader. Thank you for enjoying what I love to do so much. Your enthusiasm for crochet is what keeps me energized to share my kooky designs, so thank you very much.

Contents

Introduction

Tell me, how excited do you get when you find out that a friend or relative is expecting? Now be honest, do you get more excited about seeing the baby or about crocheting for the baby? I don't know whether I could answer that honestly myself! There is just something so fun about crocheting baby projects. I don't know whether it is the small size (you'll love how quickly they come together), the bright fun colors, or the cute factor. No matter which element it is for you, you'll find it in abundance in the pages of this book.

While writing *Blueprint Crochet: Modern Designs for the Visual Crocheter* (my first book), I knew I was only giving you a taste of how far symbol crochet can go. Now, with this book, I am combining my love of bright fun baby projects with a bit of symbol crochet education. Because these projects are small in size, they present the perfect opportunity to learn something new or just perfect techniques you already love. If your first attempt is not perfect, I'm sure your little cutie won't complain. Besides, practice makes perfect and this book provides many projects that will ease you into symbol crochet and fun techniques. Even if you are already an accomplished crocheter, you will find plenty of challenging projects that will allow you to show off your skills!

Above all, each project was designed to bring a smile to your little pumpkin's face as well as to give you tremendous crochet enjoyment. Have fun!

Symbol Crochet

In this book, you will be going on a journey deep into some really fun crochet techniques. There will be some crochet colorwork, crocheting from the neckline down, combining granny squares and stitch patterns, crocheting appliqués to add to projects, sculptural crochet, and Tunisian crochet. You will be aided in all of these techniques by symbol crochet. So, let's begin our journey by mastering all that symbol crochet has to offer.

Symbol Crochet Basics

You will see crochet symbols used throughout this book. They will help you understand the instructions by giving you a visual reference for the crochet stitches and patterns you will be using. They are quite simple to follow once you have mastered the basic concepts, so read on and discover the magic of crochet symbols. I think you'll fall in love with them just as I have!

THE SYMBOLS

The key to understanding crochet symbols is that each symbol represents a crochet stitch. I like to think of them as little stick diagrams of the actual stitch. Let's start with the smallest stitch, the chain, by looking at the crochet symbol key at right. The symbol for a chain is an oval. Why an oval? Well, think about making a chain stitch; it's a simple loop pulled through another loop. That loop, which is our chain stitch, looks a lot like an oval, doesn't it? The international crochet symbols try to mimic the actual stitch as much as possible.

Let's look at a few more; you'll soon see that reading crochet symbols becomes quite intuitive. Appearing next in the stitch key is the slip stitch, which is a filled dot—the symbol is small, almost invisible, just like the stitch. Moving on, the single crochet is a squat cross, again just like the stitch. The half double crochet is slightly taller than the single crochet. The double crochet is taller than the half double and has an extra cross in its middle. From the double crochet up, the little crosses tell you how many yarnovers you have before you insert your hook. Go ahead; make a double crochet. Now, look at your stitch. Do you see the little horizontal line in the middle of the stitch? That is why the double crochet symbol has that little bar in the middle of its post. The rest of the symbols fall in line with the same reasoning. If the stitch is short, the symbol will be short; if the stitch puffs out (like a cluster stitch), the symbol will as well.

⬭	chain
•	slip stitch
+	single crochet
T	half double crochet
⧢	double crochet
⅄	dc2tog
⬯	3dc-cl
⧣	treble crochet
⧥	double treble

Crochet Symbols

Don't worry. You won't have to memorize the symbols. A full crochet symbol key is included on page 17. In addition, there are instructions for creating the stitches provided in the glossary and also occasionally in individual patterns (where a special stitch may be used exclusively).

GRANNY SQUARE DIAGRAMS

Now, if you'd like to try out your crochet symbol-reading skills, a granny square diagram is the best way to get your feet wet. I like to think of granny square diagrams as tiny maps. They show the big picture of what the motif will look like when completed, with round-by-round directions on how to get there. Let's look at the granny square example below. To begin, you need to start in the center of the diagram, just as you would to crochet the granny square itself. Now, look at the center of the diagram; can you tell how many chains to crochet to start the motif? That's right: 7. You can see that it is 7 by looking at the circled number in the center or by counting the chain stitches surrounding it.

Granny Square Example

Here's another question for you. On Round 4 how many ch-4 sps are there? There are 12. You can tell which round is #4 by looking for the "4" at the beginning of the round or by counting the different colored rounds up from the center. Each round is a different color and is numbered to help you keep your place. You can see that Round 4 is a blue round. To find out how many ch-4 sps there are, you just count the number around. As you can see, these little maps can come in handy while you are crocheting because you can check your progress as you go.

To test your new granny square diagram-reading skills, check out Rosa Car Coat on page 65 or Kyla Mod Stroller Blanket on page 123.

STITCH PATTERN DIAGRAMS

Stitch pattern diagrams are not that different from granny square diagrams. The key difference is that, instead of crocheting in the round, you crochet back and forth in turned rows. Therefore, when you are reading the diagram, you need to start at the bottom foundation chain and crochet as many chains as the diagram shows. To do this, begin by counting the number of chains before and after the stitch pattern repeat (SR), which is the combination of stitches that are repeated for each row. When you are reading a stitch pattern diagram, you'll want to count how many chains are in one SR and then multiply that by the number of SR the pattern tells you to do and add it to the first chain count; this will give you your foundation chain count. In addition, you will see the row repeat (RR), which is the row or rows that are repeated to make up the crocheted fabric. These two indicators (SR and RR) will allow you to count the repeats rather than having to count every row or stitch.

Let's look at the stitch pattern example below. In this pattern, one dc2tog and ch-1 sp make up one SR and two dc2tog rows and two sc rows make up the RR. This project is given in four sizes; S, M, L, and XL. Let's figure out how many chains you'll need to crochet for the medium size by breaking down the information we see.

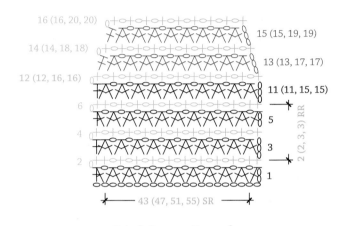

Stitch Pattern Example

First, the SR is made from 2 foundation chains. The diagram shows that there are 47 SR in the medium size. The foundation chains outside of the 47 SR equal 5 (3 before and 2 after). So here's the math: $2 \times 47 + 5 = 99$. Therefore, you chain 99 to start the body. Okay, now how many ch-1 sps will you have at the end of Row 16 of the shaping of the body? To answer this question, count how many ch-1 sps are on Row 2 of the body diagram (9). Now count how many ch-1 sps are on Row 16 of the shaping (8). We already know that our project has 47 SR to start, which means that we would have 47 ch-1 sps on our project at Row 2. Therefore, because there is one less ch-1 sp shown on the diagram at Row 16, our project would have 46 ch-1 sps.

Now, If you are looking for a project that will get you started on using symbol crochet, check out Callum Pullover (page 29), Stella Jacket (page 37), or Burp Cloth Bib (page 117).

Symbol Crochet Rules

Now that you are familiar with the basics of symbol crochet, we are going to learn some more techniques. The catch is this: the rest of the techniques break some of the rules of symbol crochet that we just learned. Here is a list of those rules for your reference.

TOP 6 RULES OF SYMBOL CROCHET

1. Each symbol represents one stitch to crochet (see page 17 for a crochet symbol key; refer to the glossary, beginning on page 146, for stitch instructions).
2. Each symbol is a tiny stick diagram of the actual stitch. The taller and/or fatter the symbol, the taller and/or fatter the stitch it represents.
3. Each row or round is a different color in the diagrams to help you keep track of which one you are working on.
4. Each row or round has a number next to the beginning turning chain to indicate the start of the row or round.
5. Granny square and motif diagrams start in the center and increase outward just as you would crochet.
6. Stitch pattern diagrams work rows back and forth and will indicate in brackets how many stitches or rows to repeat in a design.

Now that you are clear on the rules, let's break them!

Colorwork Crochet

The easiest "rule-breaking" concept to grasp in symbol crochet is crocheting colorwork. Why? Because it only breaks one of our symbol crochet rules—namely, Rule #3, because the different color of each round, row, or stitch now means that you need to change colors. How will you know that you need to change colors? Here are some clues to look for:

1. The project has lots of colors in the photograph and has multiple colors listed in the yarn section.
2. There is a color key next to the diagram, indicating, for example, that black is the main color (MC) yarn and blue is the contrasting color (CC) yarn.
3. The directions will tell you to change colors as the diagram indicates or the color changes will be called out in the instructions themselves.

Granny A

Granny B

Let's examine what a colorwork diagram looks like. At right, you see a traditional stitch diagram that would be crocheted all in one color **(Granny A)** and below it is the same diagram, but this time it is a colorwork diagram **(Granny B)**. Notice that Granny B has only the center in a contrasting color and the other 3 rounds all in black. That violates Rule #3 of symbol crochet, in which every round is supposed to be a different color. Therefore, the color distribution in Granny B is a clue that the center is supposed to be crocheted in one color and the rest in another color. Don't worry, though, you won't have to determine the difference between a traditional stitch diagram and a colorwork diagram on your own. The

projects will always include several other indicators that will tip you off to the presence of a colorwork diagram (see the clues listed on page 11).

You are now ready to hop over to Hank Vest (page 45), Charlie Vest (page 59), Hunter Pullover (page 73), and Popsicle Boots (page 95) to test your colorwork skills.

Working in the Round

One of my favorite methods of creating clothes is crocheting in the round from the top down. There is nothing better then watching a sweater grow from the neckline and work its way to the ribbing. It's like magic. Plus, you get to try it on your model as you go!

Now, let's dissect the stitch diagrams a bit to understand why they look the way they do. The best way to learn to recognize the differences between diagrams for working in the round and diagrams for working in rows is to compare them closely. Look at **Diagrams C and D** at right. In the traditional rows (Diagram C), the start of each row has a turning chain and number indicating the row. Now, take a look at the rounds (Diagram D); it also has a turning chain and a number

indicating the round. The only difference is that the turning chain and number are in the center of the diagram, not on the end. In both diagrams each row or round is a different color to help you stay on the right one. The only other difference between these diagrams is whether the rounds are turned rounds or not turned rounds. There are two ways to determine whether or not to turn. The first is, of course, the pattern; it will indicate turning where applicable. The second is to look at the turning chains in the diagram: if they lean in opposite directions, they are turned rounds, if they lean in the same direction, then they are not turned rounds (Diagram D indicates turned rounds). Both Joni Jumper (page 21) and Leah Pullover (page 51) provide opportunities to work in rounds.

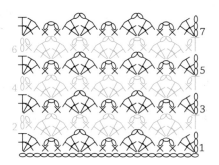

C. Working in rows

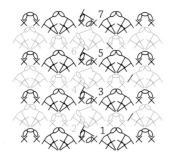

D. Working in rounds

Sculptural Crochet

Crochet is one of the coolest mediums to work in and is quite easy to learn. All the 3D crochet projects in this book are diagrammed, and you only need a few pointers to learn how to read them. When increasing—say, for an elephant's head (see Ellie on Parade, page 129)—the diagram looks exactly like a granny motif diagram. You start in the center and work your way outward. Each round has a different color to help you keep track of your place. The only difference is that your work will start to curl up into a shape instead of being flat. This shaping occurs by mixing increasing rounds with straight

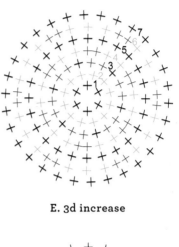

E. 3d increase

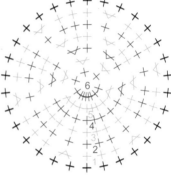

F. 3d decrease

(no increase) rounds. You cannot see the 3D effect in the diagram, but it is there when you crochet. On larger projects, the increases will be highlighted in a different color to help you visualize how many stitches there are between increases. You can see an example of this in **Diagram E** above. On Round 3 you can see that you place two sc in the first sc and one sc in the next sc, and then repeat this around. The red color of those two single crochets are just to help you see the increase more clearly. You'll probably also notice that there are no joining slip stitches and turning chains. Why is this? The project is worked in a spiral, so there is no joining at the ends of the rounds. A word of caution: not all projects will be worked in

a spiral, so you'll need to pay close attention to the instructions and the stitch diagrams for each project.

As you can see, increasing diagrams are pretty close to granny squares and easy to grasp. Decreasing diagrams, on the other hand, although not difficult, can be confusing after looking at the increasing diagrams. Take a look at **Diagram F** at left; instead of starting in the center, you will start on the outside of the diagram and work your way in (notice that the round numbers in diagram F are in the opposite orientation from those in diagram E). Each round will have fewer and fewer stitches as you work toward the center, and your project will be getting smaller as well. Other than starting at the outside and working in, the diagram is the same as a granny motif. Each round is a different color, and there is a number marking the start of a new round.

When you are ready to take this technique out for a spin, check out Pea Pod Slider Slippers (page 89), Popsicle Boots (page 95), Andy Cap (page 105), Ellie on Parade (page 129), and Robot Burt (page 135).

Baby Crochet

I'd like to touch on my philosophy of crocheting for babies. See, I come from a big family (as of writing this book, we have seventeen nieces and nephews), and there is nothing sadder to me than a baby gift that does not get used because it is too flimsy or falls apart in minutes. I have seen this happen to a lot of handmade baby gifts, and it just doesn't have to be that way. Here are my guidelines when designing a baby project, to avoid similar problems.

GUIDELINES FOR DESIGNING A BABY PROJECT

1. *Choose the right yarn for the job.*
   Whatever you do, make sure your yarn is machine washable. There is no baby alive that will not spill or spit up on your creation, so please make sure that it is easy to clean.
2. *Choose stimulating colors.*
   Babies like bright and bold colors with lots of contrast. Pastels are really difficult for them to see. So if you want your little one to squeal in delight, choose fun, bright colors. In the book, you will see that I purposely chose colors that stimulate.
3. *Choose the best style for the recipient.*
   If your kiddo is anything like my daughter, she will throw a fit if anything goes over her head. In that case, choose to make a cardigan or jacket instead of a pullover. If your baby loves cramming everything into his mouth, then choose a project that he can't reach (like Ellie on Parade, page 129) or one that can be goobered on (for example, Burp Cloth Bib, page 117). If your sweetie is tactile and likes to snuggle, then make sure you choose a project with pettable fabric (see Froggie Blanket, page 141) that her fingers won't get tangled in.
4. *Parent-proof your work.*
   Take the time to reinforce your collars with grosgrain ribbon sewn on behind the snaps. That simple trick will keep your work from getting stretched out of shape while parents wrangle the cutie into your outfit.
5. *Baby-proof your stitches.*
   Take the time to weave in your ends very securely so those little fingers do not find a way to unravel all your hard work.

How to Use This Book

The patterns are arranged within each chapter by the number of techniques used, with the fewest new techniques toward the front and the most toward the end. Within each project, the pattern is arranged into sections, each with a specific function.

THE PLANS

This section includes the schematic(s) for the project, along with the finished dimensions and other pertinent information that will help you as you move through the pattern.

DETAILS

Here you will find the details of the pattern, including special stitches and/or the stitch pattern that is the base upon which the project is built.

CONSTRUCTION

This section will walk you through the steps for shaping the details into the finished project.

FINISHING

The final section of each pattern includes the information for finishing the project with a neat, clean look.

Make sure you read through the pattern before beginning, to ensure that you understand the elements that you'll need to complete. I hope your little one will find as much joy in each new piece as you will in creating them.

Crochet Symbol Key

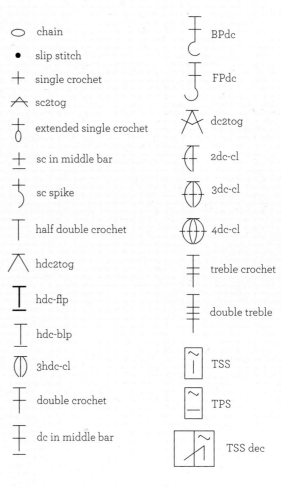

chain	BPdc
slip stitch	FPdc
single crochet	dc2tog
sc2tog	2dc-cl
extended single crochet	3dc-cl
sc in middle bar	4dc-cl
sc spike	treble crochet
half double crochet	double treble
hdc2tog	TSS
hdc-flp	TPS
hdc-blp	TSS dec
3hdc-cl	
double crochet	
dc in middle bar	

Apparel

Ever wonder why we insist on dressing baby girls in Pepto-pink frilly nightmares?
Or have you ever been surprised by the lack of cute crochet patterns for little
boys? This chapter includes myriad options presented in a rainbow of fun colors
for your little sweet pea. The garments are specifically made for ease of movement
so your little one is free to learn and play. Each design includes some twists that
will bring you deeper into symbol crochet. Not only will you learn a few new tricks
but also you'll find something to please even the pickiest parent.

joni Jumper

I am always on the lookout for clothes that can grow with my daughter. Our favorites are sleeveless dresses that can go from summer sundresses to winter tunics (when paired with a long-sleeved top and leggings). This jumper is modeled after one of our most-loved dresses. The flower appliqué adds a pop of color and feminine flair. You may find yourself making several of these for a special little girl in your life, so get creative and try different colors and appliqués!

Equipment

YARN: DK weight (#3 Light).

Shown: Classic Elite Yarns, Provence (100% mercerized Egyptian cotton; 205 yd [187 m]/3.5 oz [100 g]): #2624 deep sea (MC), 4 (5, 5, 6) hanks; #2698 orange peel (CC1), 1 (1, 1, 1) hank; #2650 new moon (CC2), 1 (1, 1, 1) hank.

HOOK: G/7 (4.50 mm), H/8 (5.00 mm), and I/9 (5.50 mm) or hooks needed to obtain gauge.

NOTIONS: Tapestry needle for weaving in ends; spray bottle with water and straight pins for blocking; two 1¼" (3.2 cm) buttons (shown: natural wood).

Gauge

24 sts (8 SR) by 15 rows = 4" × 3¾" (10 × 9.5 cm) in Poppy Stitch Pattern (psp) with G/7 hook.

21 sts (7 SR) by 15 rows = 4" × 4" (10 × 10 cm) in Poppy Stitch Pattern (psp) with I/9 hook.

Finished Size

Small (Medium, Large, Extra Large) jumper is sized to fit 6 (12, 18, 24) mths with a relaxed fit. Jumper shown is a size Medium (12 mths).

Finished Chest: 18 (20, 21, 22)" (46.5 [51, 53.5, 56] cm).

Finished Length: 17 (18, 20¾, 21¾)" (43 [45.5, 52.5, 55] cm).

The Plans

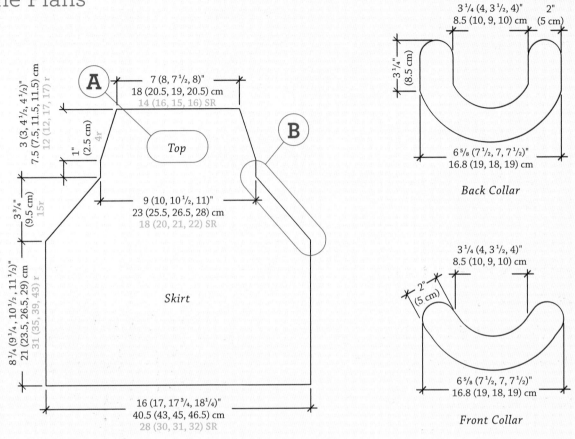

3 (3, 4½, 4½)"
7.5 (7.5, 11.5, 11.5) cm
12 (12, 17, 17) r

A

7 (8, 7½, 8)"
18 (20.5, 19, 20.5) cm
14 (16, 15, 16) SR

1" (2.5 cm)
4r

Top

B

9 (10, 10½, 11)"
23 (25.5, 26.5, 28) cm
18 (20, 21, 22) SR

3¾" (9.5 cm)
15r

Skirt

8¼ (9¼, 10½, 11½)"
21 (23.5, 26.5, 29) cm
31 (35, 39, 43) r

16 (17, 17¾, 18¼)"
40.5 (43, 45, 46.5) cm
28 (30, 31, 32) SR

3¼ (4, 3½, 4)"
8.5 (10, 9, 10) cm

2" (5 cm)

3¼" (8.5 cm)

6⅝ (7½, 7, 7½)"
16.8 (19, 18, 19) cm

Back Collar

3¼ (4, 3½, 4)"
8.5 (10, 9, 10) cm

2" (5 cm)

6⅝ (7½, 7, 7½)"
16.8 (19, 18, 19) cm

Front Collar

 NOTES:

Stitch pattern is reversible.

When instructed to work a stitch in the middle bar, insert your hook into the middle bar of the right side of the dtr stitch which is formed by the yarnover in the dtr stitch.

Details

POPPY STITCH PATTERN (PSP)

See **Poppy Stitch Pattern** diagram below for assistance.

Ch 24.

Row 1: Sc in 2nd ch from hook, ch 2, sc in next ch, *sk 1 ch, sc in next ch, ch 2, sc in next ch, rep from * across, turn—16 sc, 8 SR.

Row 2: Ch 1, (sc, ch 2, sc) in ea ch-2 sp across, turn. Rep Row 2 for pattern.

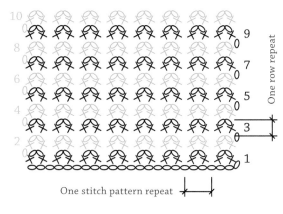

Poppy Stitch Pattern (psp)

Construction

TOP (MAKE 2)

Ch 42 (48, 45, 48) with MC and G/7 (4.5 mm) hook.

Row 1: Sc in 2nd ch from hook, ch 2, sc in next ch, *sk 1 ch, sc in next ch, ch 2, sc in next ch, rep from * across, turn—28 (32, 30, 32) sc; 14 (16, 15, 16) SR.

Row 2 (S/M only): Ch 1, (sc, ch 2, sc) in ea ch-2 sp across, turn.

TOP INCREASE:

Refer to **Stitch Diagram A** below for assistance.

Row 1: Ch 3 (counts as dc), cont in psp across, dc in last sc, turn—14 (16, 15, 16) SR.

Row 2: Ch 2 (counts as hdc), sc in dc, cont in psp across, (sc, hdc) in top of tch, turn.

Row 3: Rep Row 2.

Row 4: Ch 1, (sc, ch 2, sc) in hdc, cont in psp across, (sc, ch 2, sc) in top of tch, turn—16 (18, 17, 18) SR.

Rows 5–6: Cont in psp across, turn.

(S/M only) Rep Rows 1–4—18 (20) SR.

(L/XL only) Rep Rows 1–6. Rep Rows 1–4 once more—21 (22) SR.

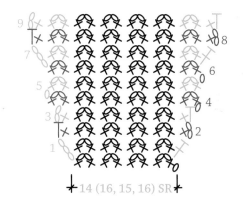

A. Top Increase

Joining Top:

Rnd 1: Ch 1, cont in psp across to end of first panel, cont in psp across second panel, sl st to first sc, turn—36 (40, 42, 44) SR.

Rnd 2: Ch 1, cont in psp around, sl st to first sc, turn. Rep Rnd 2 twice.

SKIRT

Skirt Increase:

See **Stitch Diagram B** below for assistance.

Switch to H/8 (5.00 mm) hook.

Rnd 1: Ch 1, cont in psp around, sl st to first sc, turn.

Rnd 2: Rep Rnd 1.

Rnd 3: Ch 1, cont in psp for 2 SR, (sc, ch 2, sc, ch 2, sc) in next ch-2 sp, cont in psp for 18 (20, 21, 22) SR, (sc, ch 2, sc, ch 2, sc) in next ch-2 sp, cont in psp to end, sl st to first sc, turn.

Rnds 4–5: Rep Rnd 1—38 (42, 44, 46) SR.

Rep Rnds 3–5 three times. Rep Rnd 3 once—46 (50, 52, 54) SR.

Switch to I/9 (5.50 mm) hook.

Rep Rnd 1 thirty (thirty-four, thirty-eight, forty-two) times.

Last Rnd (RS): Ch 1, 3 sc in ea ch-2 sp around, sl st to first sc, fasten off.

ARM EDGING

Join MC to RS edge of arm with G/7 (4.50 mm) hook. Ch 1, sc evenly around arm opening, along ends of rows to opp side, sl st to first sc, fasten off, weave in ends. Rep on opp arm opening.

Diagram B. Skirt Increase

Back Collar

Ch 60, (65, 62, 65), with CC2 and G/7 (4.50 mm) hook.

Rnd 1: Sc in 10th ch from hook, sc in next 10 ch, 2 sc in next ch, sc in next 27 (32, 29, 32) ch, 2 sc in next ch, sc in next 11 ch, ch 9, turn work 180 degrees (beg working in free lps of foundation ch), sc in next 11 ch, sk next ch, sc in next 27 (32, 29, 32) ch, sk next ch, sc in next 11 ch, do not turn—102 (112, 106, 112) sc.

Rnd 2: 11 sc in ch-sp, sc in next 18 sc, 2 sc in next sc, sc in next 7 (10, 8, 10) sc, 2 sc in next sc, sc in next 7 (9, 8, 9) sc, 2 sc in next sc, sc in next 18 sc, 11 sc in ch-sp, sc in next 11 sc, sc2tog over next 2 sc, sc in next 23 (28, 25, 28) sc, sc2tog over next 2 sc, sc in next 11 sc, do not turn—125 (135, 129, 135) sc.

Rnd 3: Sc in next 4 sc, 2 sc in next 3 sc, sc in next 24 sc, 2 sc in next sc, sc in next 14 (19, 16, 19) sc, 2 sc in next sc, sc in next 24 sc, 2 sc in next 3 sc, sc in next 15 sc, sc2tog over next 2 sc, sc in next 4 (6, 5, 6) sc, sc2tog over next 2 sc, sc in next 10 sc, sc2tog over next 2 sc, sc in next 4 (7, 5, 7) sc, sc2tog over next 2 sc, sc in next 10 sc, do not turn—129 (139, 133, 139) sc.

Rnd 4: Sc in next 4 sc, *sc in next sc, 2 sc in next sc*, rep from * to * twice, sc in next 17 sc, 2 sc in next sc, sc in next 14 (17, 15, 17), 2 sc in next sc, sc in next 15 (17, 16, 17) sc, 2 sc in next sc, sc in next 17 sc, **2 sc in next sc, sc in next sc**, rep from ** to ** twice, sc in next 15 sc, sc2tog over next 2 sc, sc in next 8 (10, 9, 10), sc2tog over next 2 sc, sc in next 7 (10, 8, 10), sc2tog over next 2 sc, sc in next 11 sc, do not turn—135 (145, 135, 145) sc.

Rnd 5: Sc in next 4 sc, *sc in next 2 sc, 2 sc in next sc, sc in next sc*, rep from * to * twice, sc in next 27 (29, 28, 29) sc, 2 sc in next sc, sc in next 13 (14, 13, 14) sc, 2 sc in next

sc, sc in next 27 (29, 28, 29) sc, **sc in next sc, 2 sc in next sc, sc in next sc**, rep from ** to ** twice, sc in next 15 sc, sc2tog over next 2 sc, sc in next 3 (5, 4, 5) sc, sc2tog over next 2 sc, sc in next 4 (5, 4, 5), sc2tog over next 2 sc, sc in next 3 (5, 4, 5), sc2tog over next 2 sc, sc in next 8 sc, sl st to first sc, fasten off—142 (152, 146, 152) sc.

FRONT COLLAR

Ch 36, (41, 38, 41), with CC1 and G/7 (4.50 mm) hook.

Rnd 1: Sc in 2nd ch from hook, sc in next 2 ch, 2 sc in next ch, sc in next 27 (32, 29, 32) ch, 2 sc in next ch, sc in next 2 ch, 3 sc in last ch, turn work 180 degrees (beg working in free lps of foundation ch), sc in next 2 ch, sk next ch, sc in next 27 (32, 29, 32) ch, sk next ch, sc in next 2 ch, 2 sc in last ch, do not turn—72 (82, 76, 82) sc.

Rnd 2: 2 sc in first sc, sc in next 9 sc, 2 sc in next sc, sc in next 7 (10, 8, 10) sc, 2 sc in next sc, sc in next 7 (9, 8, 9) sc, 2 sc in next sc, sc in next 9 sc, 2 sc in next 3 sc, sc in next 2 sc, sc2tog over next 2 sc, sc in next 23 (28, 25, 28) sc, sc2tog over next 2 sc, sc in next 2 sc, 2 sc in next 2 sc, do not turn—79 (89, 83, 89) sc.

Rnd 3: 2 sc in first sc, sc in next 12 sc, 2 sc in next sc, sc in next 14 (19, 16, 19) sc, 2 sc in next sc, sc in next 11 sc, *2 sc in next sc, sc in next sc*, rep from * to * twice, sc in next 2 sc, sc2tog over next 2 sc, sc in next 4 (6, 5, 6) sc, sc2tog over next 2 sc, sc in next 10 sc, sc2tog over next 2 sc, sc in next 4

(7, 5, 7) sc, sc2tog over next 2 sc, sc in next 2 sc, rep from * to * once, 2 sc in next sc, do not turn—83 (93, 87, 93) sc.

Rnd 4: Sc in next sc, 2 sc in next sc, sc in next 5 sc, 2 sc in next sc, sc in next 14 (17, 15, 17), 2 sc in next sc, sc in next 15 (17, 16, 17) sc, 2 sc in next sc, sc in next 4 sc, *sc in next sc, 2 sc in next sc, sc in next sc*, rep from * to * twice, sc in next 2 sc, sc2tog over next 2 sc, sc in next 8 (10, 9, 10), sc2tog over next 2 sc, sc in next 7 (10, 8, 10), sc2tog over next 2 sc, sc in next 2 sc, rep from * to * twice, do not turn—89 (99, 93, 99) sc.

Rnd 5: Sc in next 2 sc, 2 sc in next sc, sc in next 15 (17, 16, 17) sc, 2 sc in next sc, sc in next 13 (14, 13, 14) sc, 2 sc in next sc, sc in next 14 (16, 15, 16) sc, *sc in next 2 sc, 2 sc in next sc, sc in next sc*, rep from * to * twice, sc in next 2 sc, sc2tog over next 2 sc, sc in next 3 (5, 4, 5) sc, sc2tog over next 2 sc, sc in next 4 (5, 4, 5) sc, sc2tog over next 2 sc, sc in next 3 (5, 4, 5) sc, sc2tog over next 2 sc, sc in next 2 sc, rep from * to * twice, sl st to first sc, fasten off—93 (103, 97, 103) sc.

Finishing

BLOCKING AND SEAMING

Pin dress and collars to schematic size (see The Plans on page 22). Spritz with water and allow to dry. Pin Front Collar to RS of dress. Backstitch collar to dress with matching yarn. Rep with Back Collar on back of dress. Sew buttons to top of front collar, attaching one button about 1" (2.5 cm) from each end.

FLOWER APPLIQUÉ

Crochet flower appliqué, referring to **Stitch Diagram C** at right.

With CC2, ch 8, sl st to first ch to form ring.

Rnd 1 (RS): Ch 1, sc in ring 16 times, sl st to first sc, do not turn—16 sc.

Rnd 2: Ch 5, *sk next sc, dtr in next sc, ch 4, dc in middle bar of dtr, rep from * around, dc in 3rd ch of tch, ch 2, hdc in 5th ch of tch, fasten off CC2, do not turn—7 ch-4 sps.

Rnd 3: Join CC1, ch 1, 3 sc around post of hdc, *ch 3, 5 sc in next ch-4 sp, rep from * around, ch 3, 2 sc in ch-2 sp, sl st to first sc, do not turn—40 sc.

Rnd 4: Ch 5, *dtr in next ch-3 sp, ch 4, dc in middle bar of dtr, sk 2 sc, dtr in next sc, ch 4, dc in middle bar of dtr, rep from * around, dtr in next ch-3 sp, ch 4, dc in middle bar of dtr, dc in 3rd ch of tch, ch 2, hdc in 5th ch of tch, do not turn—15 ch-4 sps.

Rnd 5: Ch 1, 3 sc around post of hdc, *(3 sc, ch 2, 3 sc) in next ch-4 sp, 6 sc in next ch-4 sp, rep from * around, (3 sc, ch 2, 3 sc) in next ch-4 sp, 3 sc in ch-sp, sl st to first sc, fasten off—96 sc.

With matching yarn and tapestry needle, sew flower to lower left-hand side of front of dress, about 1¼" (3 cm) above bottom edge and flush with side edge of front.

C. Flower Diagram

callum
Pullover

This simple embellished pullover is perfect for warming up any little one. The shape and style will work for either girls or boys and can easily be customized with a quick color change. Use the included instructions to create the dino appliqué or mix and match your favorite appliqués and buttons to decorate it especially for your little pumpkin.

Equipment

YARN: DK weight (#3 Light).

Shown: Classic Elite, Pebbles (75% cotton, 25% acrylic; 110 yd [100.5 m]/1.7 oz [50 g]): #2888 life jacket (MC), 4 (5, 6, 7) balls; #2885 port (CC1), 2 (2, 2, 2) balls; #2850 butter yellow (CC2), 1 (1, 1, 1) balls.

HOOK: G/7 (4.5 mm) or hook needed to obtain gauge.

NOTIONS: Tapestry needle for weaving in ends; two ⅝" (1.5 cm) buttons; 2 small sew-on snaps (shown: ⅜" [1 cm]); handsewing needle and matching sewing thread; 5" (12.5 cm) of ½" (1.3 cm) wide grosgrain ribbon (for stabilizing snaps); spray bottle with water and straight pins for blocking.

Gauge

16 hdc by 14 rows = 4" × 4" (10 × 10 cm) in Offset Stitch Pattern (osp).

Finished Size

Small (Medium, Large, Extra Large) pullover is sized to fit 6 (12, 18, 24) mths with a relaxed fit. Sample shown is a size Medium (12 mths).

Finished Chest: 21½ (24, 26½, 29)" (54.5 [61, 67.5, 73.5] cm).

Finished Length: 8¼ (9¼, 11¼, 12¼)" (21 [23.5, 28.5, 31] cm).

The Plans

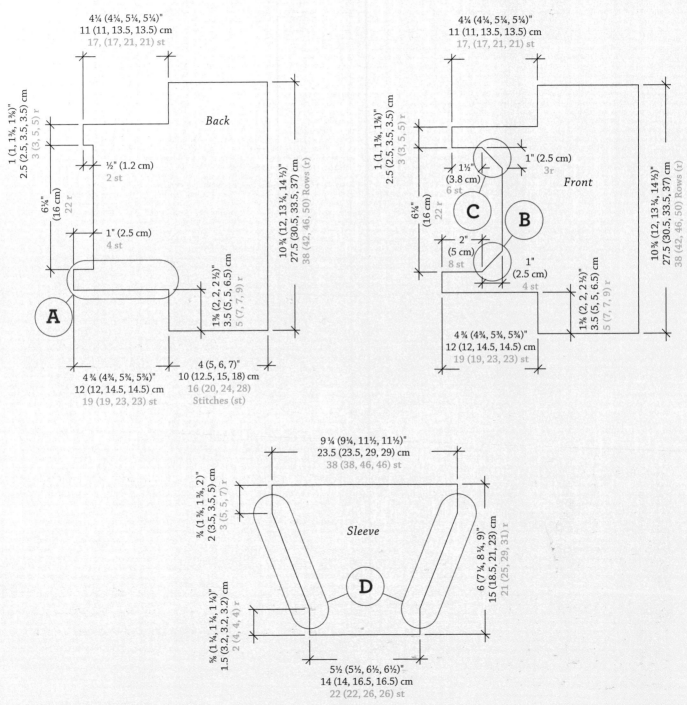

4¼ (4¼, 5¼, 5¼)"
11 (11, 13.5, 13.5) cm
17, (17, 21, 21) st

Back

1 (1, 1⅜, 1⅜)"
2.5 (2.5, 3.5, 3.5) cm
3 (3, 5, 5) r

½" (1.2 cm)
2 st

6¼"
(16 cm)
22 r

1" (2.5 cm)
4 st

10¾ (12, 13¼, 14½)"
27.5 (42, 46, 50) Rows (r)

1⅜ (2, 2, 2½)"
3.5 (5, 5, 6.5) cm
5 (7, 7, 9) r

A

4¾ (4¾, 5¾, 5¾)"
12 (12, 14.5, 14.5) cm
19 (19, 23, 23) st

4 (5, 6, 7)"
10 (12.5, 15, 18) cm
16 (20, 24, 28)
Stitches (st)

4¼ (4¼, 5¼, 5¼)"
11 (11, 13.5, 13.5) cm
17, (17, 21, 21) st

Front

1 (1, 1⅜, 1⅜)"
2.5 (2.5, 3.5, 3.5) cm
3 (3, 5, 5) r

1½"
(3.8 cm)
6 st

1" (2.5 cm)
3 r

C

B

6¼"
(16 cm)
22 r

2"
(5 cm)
8 st

1"
(2.5 cm)
4 st

10¾ (12, 13¼, 14½)"
27.5 (42, 46, 50) Rows (r)

1⅜ (2, 2, 2½)"
3.5 (5, 5, 6.5) cm
5 (7, 7, 9) r

4¾ (4¾, 5¾, 5¾)"
12 (12, 14.5, 14.5) cm
19 (19, 23, 23) st

9¼ (9¼, 11½, 11½)"
23.5 (23.5, 29, 29) cm
38 (38, 46, 46) st

Sleeve

¾ (1⅜, 1⅜, 2)"
2 (3.5, 3.5, 5) cm
3 (5, 5, 7) r

⅝ (1¼, 1¼, 1¼)"
1.5 (3.2, 3.2, 3.2) cm
2 (4, 4, 4) r

D

6 (7¼, 8¼, 9)"
15 (18.5, 21, 23) cm
21 (25, 29, 31) r

5½ (5½, 6½, 6½)"
14 (14, 16.5, 16.5) cm
22 (22, 26, 26) st

Details

OFFSET STITCH PATTERN (OSP)

See **Offset Stitch Pattern** diagram below for assistance.

Ch 18.

Row 1(RS): Hdc in 3rd ch from hook (skipped 2 ch count as hdc), hdc in ea ch across, turn—17 hdc.

Row 2: Ch 2, hdc bet next 2 hdc across to end, turn.

Rep Row 2 for pattern.

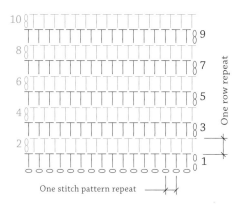

Offset Stitch Pattern (osp)

Construction

BACK

Ch 17 (21, 25, 29) with MC.

Row 1(RS): Hdc in 3rd ch from hook (skipped 2 ch count as hdc), hdc in ea ch across, turn—16 (20, 24, 28) hdc.

Rep Row 2 of osp 4 (6, 6, 8) times.

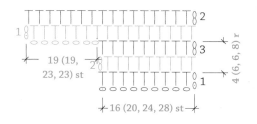

A. Armhole

Armhole Opening and Shoulder:

See **Stitch Diagram A** above for assistance.

Row 1: Ch 21 (21, 25, 25), hdc in 3rd ch from hook, hdc in ea ch across, hdc between next 2 hdc across to end, turn—35 (39, 47, 51) hdc.

Rep Row 2 of osp 2 (2, 4, 4) times.

Neck Opening:

Row 1: Cont in Row 2 of osp across for 31 (35, 43, 47) hdc total, turn.

Rep Row 2 of osp 21 times.

Opposite Shoulder:

Row 1: Lay down working yarn, join new ball with sl st to top of tch at beg of prev row, ch 2, fasten off, pick up working yarn, cont in Row 2 of osp across, hdc in ea ch across, turn—33 (37, 45, 49) hdc.

Rep Row 2 of osp 2 (2, 4, 4) times, fasten off.

Opposite Arm Opening:

Row 1: Sk 17 (17, 21, 21) hdc, join yarn with sl st bet next 2 hdc, ch 2 (counts as hdc), cont in Row 2 of osp across to end, turn—16 (20, 24, 28) hdc.

Rep Row 2 of osp 4 (6, 6, 8) times, fasten off.

FRONT

Cont with Back directions to Neck Opening.

Neck Opening:

See **Stitch Diagram B** at right for assistance.

Row 1: Cont in Row 2 of osp across for 24 (28, 36, 40) hdc total, sc bet next 2 hdc, sl st bet next 2 hdc, turn.

Row 2: Sk sl st, sl st in sc, sc in first hdc, cont in Row 2 of osp to end, turn—23 (27, 35, 39) hdc.

Row 3: Cont in Row 2 of osp to last hdc, sc in last hdc, sl st in sc, turn.

Row 4: Sk sl st, sl st in sc, ch 2 (counts as hdc), cont in Row 2 of osp to end, turn.

Rep Row 2 of osp 15 times.

Opposite Neck Opening and Shoulder:

See **Stitch Diagram C** at right for assistance.

Row 1: Ch 3 (counts as hdc), hdc in 3rd ch from hook, cont in Row 2 of osp across to end, turn—24 (28, 36, 40) hdc.

Row 2: Cont in Row 2 of osp to tch, (hdc, dc) in top of tch, turn—26 (30, 38, 42) sts.

Row 3: Rep Row 1 of Opposite Neck Opening—27 (31, 39, 43) hdc.

Row 4: Lay down working yarn, join new ball with sl st top of tch at beg of prev row, ch 6, fasten off, pick up work-

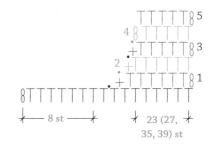

B. Neck Opening

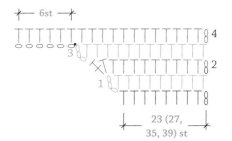

C. Opposite Neck Opening

ing yarn, cont in Row 2 of osp across, hdc in ea ch across, turn—33 (37, 45, 49) hdc.

Rep Row 2 of osp 2 (2, 4, 4) times, fasten off.

Opposite Arm Opening:

Cont with Back directions to end.

SLEEVE (MAKE 2)

Ch 23 (23, 27, 27) with MC.

Row 1(RS): Hdc in 3rd ch from hook (sk ch count as hdc), hdc in ea ch across, turn—22 (22, 26, 26) hdc.

Rep Row 2 of osp 1 (3, 3, 3) time(s).

Arm Increase:

See **Stitch Diagram D** at right for assistance.

Row 1: Ch 3 (counts as hdc), hdc in 3rd ch from hook, cont in Row 2 of osp across to tch, hdc in top of tch, turn—24 (24, 28, 28) hdc.

Row 2: Cont in Row 2 of osp, turn.

Rep Row 1–2 of Arm Increase 7 (7, 9, 9) times.

Rep Row 2 of osp 3 (5, 5, 7) times, fasten off.

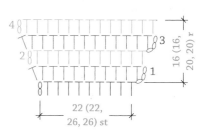

D. Arm Increase

Finishing

BLOCKING AND SEAMING

Pin Back, Front, and Sleeves to schematic measurements. Spritz with water and allow to dry. Pin right sides of Front and Back together. Whipstitch side seams together with leftover yarn. Seam left shoulder by sl st through both fabrics at once. Turn pullover RS out.

BOTTOM EDGING

Join MC with sl st to Back bottom edge, ch 11.

Row 1: Sc in 2nd ch from hook and each ch across, sl st in each of next 2 sts on body (first sl st joins ribbing to body, second counts as a tch), turn—10 sc.

Row 2: Sc-blp in each sc across, turn.

Row 3: Ch 1, sc-blp in ea sc across, sl st in each of next 2 sts on body, turn.

Rep Rows 2–3 evenly around body, fasten off, weave in ends. With tapestry needle, whipstitch ribbing seams together.

COLLAR

Join CC1 with WS facing at edge of Back right shoulder with sl st.

Row 1: Ch 1, sc evenly across shoulder, 3 sc on outside corner, sc evenly around Back and Front neck, 3 sc on outside corner, sc evenly across Front shoulder, turn.

Row 2: Ch 1, sc evenly around shoulder and neck edge, 3 sc on outside corners, sk 1 sc on inside corners, turn.

Rep Row 2 twice, fasten off.

SLEEVE SEAMING AND CUFFS

Pin Sleeves to Back and Front panels with RS facing (overlap collar on right shoulder before pinning sleeve). Whipstitch armhole and underarm seams tog with leftover yarn. Turn right side out. Join MC with sl st to cuff at seam, follow directions for Bottom Edging around.

BUTTONS AND SNAPS

Sew buttons to RS of right shoulder for decoration, leaving a gap, about ¼–½" (6 mm–1.3 cm) wide between the buttons. Cut the grosgrain ribbon in half. Then, using the thread and handsewing needle, sew one half of each snap to each piece of ribbon securely, centering them and leaving the same gap between the snaps as you left between the buttons. Sew grosgrain ribbon with snaps to inside of collar, corresponding to the placement of the buttons. Be sure to fold under the short edges of the grosgrain ribbon as you stitch it down to hide the raw edges.

DINO APPLIQUÉ

Referring to **Stitch Diagram E** below for assistance, crochet Dino body with CC1 for 13 rows, fasten off.

Join CC1 to Dino at Row 10 with sl st to sc2tog. Follow Stitch Diagram E below for Rows 14–20, fasten off. Join CC1 to Dino at Row 3 with a sl st in the 4th ch as shown. Follow Stitch Diagram E for Rows 21–22, do not turn.

Last Rnd: Sc evenly around entire Dino, 2 sc in outside corners, sl st to first sc, fasten off, leave long tail for sewing.

Referring to **Stitch Diagram F** at right for assistance, join CC2 with sl st to Dino body, 2 sc from edge of tail.

Row 1: Sc in next 2 sc, sl st in next sc, turn.

Row 2: Ch 1, sk sl st, sc2tog over 2 sc, fasten off. Join CC2, in same sc as last sl st on prev scale row.

Row 3: Sc in next 3 sc, sl st in next sc, turn.

Row 4: Ch 1, sk sl st, sc2tog in next 2 sc, sc2tog in prev sc and next sc, turn.

Row 5: Ch 1, sc2tog in next 2 sc2tog, fasten off.

Rows 6–8: Join CC2, in same sc as last sl st on Row 3, Rep Rows 3–5.

Rows 9–11: Join CC2, in same sc as last sl st on Row 6, Rep Rows 3–5.

Rows 12–13: Join CC2, in same sc as last sl st on Row 9, Rep Rows 1–2.

Using yarn tails, sew completed Dino appliqué to right-hand side of pullover Front near the Bottom Edging (see photo on page 28 for placement), using small whipstitches around the edge of the Dino.

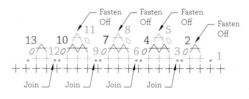

F. Scales Stitch Pattern

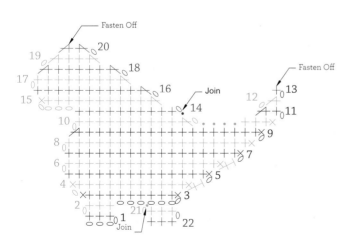

E. Dino Stitch Pattern

stella
Jacket

Do you know a little girl who is one part mischief and one part sugar and spice, with just the right amount of sparkle in her eyes? Well, this jacket is for her. The Asian flair of the frog closures mixed with the bright and fun color combination makes this jacket adorable and fun to wear. The jacket is made from acrylic yarn that is easy to wash and lightweight, making this a versatile jacket that can be worn from spring through fall.

Equipment

YARN: DK weight (#3 Light).

Shown: Red Heart, Designer Sport (100% acrylic; 279 yd [255.1 m]/3 oz [85 g]): #3801 aqua ice (MC), 2 (2, 2, 3) balls; #3690 bay leaf (CC), 1 (1, 1, 1) ball.

HOOK: H/8 (5.00 mm) or hook needed to obtain gauge; G/6 (4.25 mm) for Frog Closures.

NOTIONS: Tapestry needle for weaving in ends; spray bottle with water and straight pins for blocking.

Gauge

16 sts (8 SR) by 13 rows = 4" × 4" (10 × 10 cm) in Crumple Stitch Pattern (csp).

Finished Size

Small (Medium, Large, Extra Large) jacket is sized to fit 6 (12, 18, 24) mths with a relaxed fit. Jacket shown is a size Extra Large (28 mths).

Finished chest: 22 (24, 26, 28)" (56 [61, 66, 71] cm).

Finished length: 10⅜ (10⅞, 13¼, 14)" (26.5 [27.5, 33.5, 35.5] cm).

The Plans

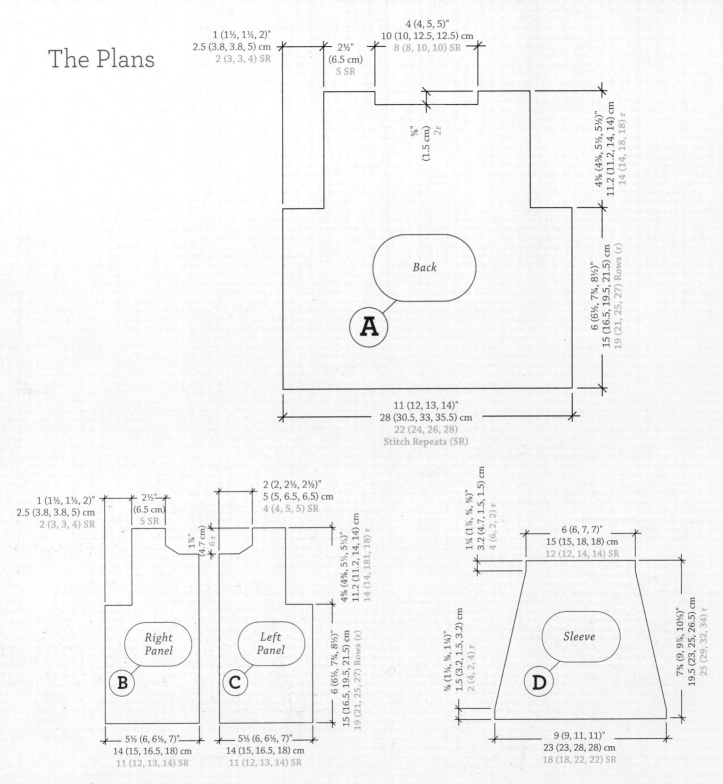

1 (1½, 1½, 2)"
2.5 (3.8, 3.8, 5) cm
2 (3, 3, 4) SR

2½"
(6.5 cm)
5 SR

4 (4, 5, 5)"
10 (10, 12.5, 12.5) cm
8 (8, 10, 10) SR

⅝"
(1.5 cm)
2r

4⅜ (4⅜, 5½, 5½)"
11.2 (11.2, 14, 14) cm
14 (14, 18, 18) r

Back

A

6 (6½, 7¾, 8½)"
15 (16.5, 19.5, 21.5) cm
19 (21, 25, 27) Rows (r)

11 (12, 13, 14)"
28 (30.5, 33, 35.5) cm
22 (24, 26, 28)
Stitch Repeats (SR)

1 (1½, 1½, 2)"
2.5 (3.8, 3.8, 5) cm
2 (3, 3, 4) SR

2½"
(6.5 cm)
5 SR

1⅞"
(4.7 cm)
6 r

Right Panel

B

2 (2, 2½, 2½)"
5 (5, 6.5, 6.5) cm
4 (4, 5, 5) SR

4⅜ (4⅜, 5½, 5½)"
11.2 (11.2, 14, 14) cm
14 (14, 181, 18) r

Left Panel

C

6 (6½, 7¾, 8½)"
15 (16.5, 19.5, 21.5) cm
19 (21, 25, 27) Rows (r)

5½ (6, 6½, 7)"
14 (15, 16.5, 18) cm
11 (12, 13, 14) SR

5½ (6, 6½, 7)"
14 (15, 16.5, 18) cm
11 (12, 13, 14) SR

1¼ (1⅞, ⅝, ⅝)"
3.2 (4.7, 1.5, 1.5) cm
4 (6, 2, 2) r

6 (6, 7, 7)"
15 (15, 18, 18) cm
12 (12, 14, 14) SR

Sleeve

D

⅝ (1¼, ⅝, 1¼)"
1.5 (3.2, 1.5, 3.2) cm
2 (4, 2, 4) r

7¾ (9, 9⅞, 10½)"
19.5 (23, 25, 26.5) cm
25 (29, 32, 34) r

9 (9, 11, 11)"
23 (23, 28, 28) cm
18 (18, 22, 22) SR

Details

CRUMPLE STITCH PATTERN (CSP)

See **Crumple Stitch Pattern** diagram below for assistance.

Ch 19.

Row 1(RS): (Sc, dc) in 4th ch from hook (skipped ch count as hdc), *sk 1 ch, (sc, dc) in next ch, rep from * across to last ch, hdc in last ch, turn—18 sts; 8 SR.

Row 2: Ch 2 (count as hdc), *(sc, dc) in next sc and in each sc across (sk all dc), hdc in top of tch, turn.

Rep Row 2 for pattern.

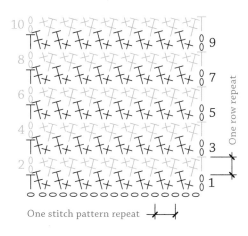

Crumple Stitch Pattern (csp)

Construction

BACK

Refer to **Stitch Diagram A** below for assistance.

Ch 47 (51, 55, 59) with MC.

Row 1(RS): (Sc, dc) in 4th ch from hook (skipped ch count as hdc), *sk 1 ch, (sc, dc) in next ch, rep from * across to last ch, hdc in last ch, turn—46 (50, 54, 58) sts; 22 (24, 26, 28) SR.
Rep Row 2 of csp 18 (20, 24, 26) times.

Armhole Opening:

Row 1: Sl st in next 5 (7, 7, 9) sts, ch 2, cont in csp across to last 2 (3, 3, 4) sc, hdc in next dc, turn—18 (18, 20, 20) SR.
Rep Row 2 of csp 11 (11, 15, 15) times.

Shoulders:

Row 1a: Cont in Row 2 of csp across for 5 sc total, hdc in next dc, turn—12 sts; 5 SR.

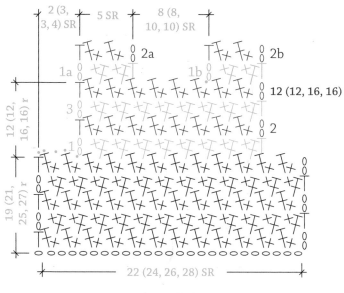

A. Back Panel Shaping

Rep Row 2 of csp once, fasten off.

Row 1b: Sk 7 (7, 9, 9) sc, join MC with sl st in next sc, ch 2 (counts as hdc), cont in Row 2 of csp across to end, turn—12 sts; 5 SR.

Rep Row 2 of csp once, fasten off.

RIGHT FRONT

Refer to **Stitch Diagram B** below for assistance.

Ch 25 (27, 29, 31) with MC.

Row 1(RS): (Sc, dc) in 4th ch from hook (skipped ch count as hdc), *sk 1 ch, (sc, dc) in next ch, rep from * across to last ch, hdc in last ch, turn—24 (26, 28, 30) sts; 11 (12, 13, 14) SR.

Rep Row 2 of csp 18 (20, 24, 26) times.

Armhole Opening:

Starting with Row 1, follow Stitch Diagram B below for 8 (8, 12, 12) rows.

Neck Opening:

Refer to Stitch Diagram B for assistance.

Row 1: Cont in Row 2 of csp across for 6 sc total, sc in next sc, sl st in next dc, turn—15 sts; 6 SR.

Row 2: Sk sl st, sl st in next sc, sl st in next dc, cont in csp across to end, turn.

Row 3: Cont in csp across for 5 sc total, hdc in next dc, turn—12 sts; 5 SR.

Rep Row 2 of csp 4 times, fasten off.

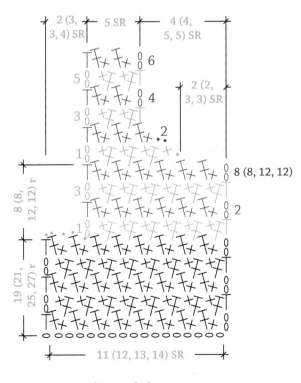

B. Right Panel Shaping

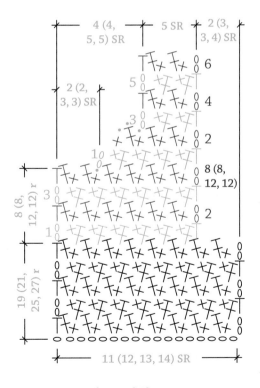

C. Left Panel Shaping

LEFT FRONT

Refer to **Stitch Diagram C** on page 40 for assistance.

Ch 25 (27, 29, 31) with MC.

Row 1(RS): (Sc, dc) in 4th ch from hook (skipped ch count as hdc), *sk 1 ch, (sc, dc) in next ch, rep from * across to last ch, hdc in last ch, turn—24 (26, 28, 30) sts; 11 (12, 13, 14) SR.

Rep Row 2 of csp 18 (20, 24, 26) times.

Armhole Opening:

Starting with Row 1, follow Stitch Diagram C on page 40 for 8 (8, 12, 12) rows, fasten off.

Neck Opening:

Refer to Stitch Diagram C for assistance.

Row 1: Sk 1 (1, 2, 2) sc, join MC with sl st in next sc, ch 2 (count as hdc) cont in csp across to end, turn—16 sts; 7 SR.

Row 2: Cont in csp across to last sc, sc in last sc, turn—14 sts; 6 SR.

Row 3: Sl st in next 3 sts, ch 2 (counts as hdc), cont in csp across to end, turn—5 SR.

Rep Row 2 of csp 3 times, fasten off.

SLEEVE (MAKE 2)

Ch 39 (39, 47, 47) with MC.

Row 1(RS): (Sc, dc) in 4th ch from hook (skipped ch count as hdc), *sk 1 ch, (sc, dc) in next ch, rep from * across to last ch, hdc in last ch, turn—38 (38, 46, 46) sts; 18 (18, 22, 22) SR.

Rep Row 2 of csp 1 (3, 1, 3) times.

Sleeve Decrease:

See **Stitch Diagram D**, above right, for assistance.

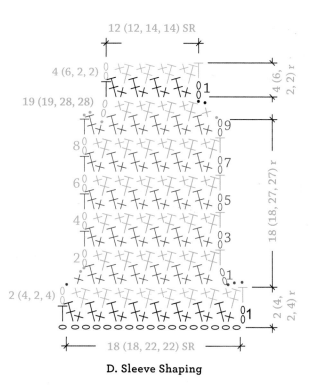

D. Sleeve Shaping

Row 1: Sl st in next 3 sts, ch 2 (counts as hdc), cont in csp across to last sc, sc in last sc, sl st in top of tch, turn—16 (16, 20, 20) SR.

Row 2: Sk sl st, sl st in next 2 sts, ch 2 (count as hdc), cont in csp across to end, turn.

Rows 3–9: Rep Row 2 of csp.

Rep Rows 1–9 of Sleeve Decrease 1 (1, 2, 2) times.

Rep Row 1 of Sleeve Decrease once more.

Sleeve Cap:

Row 1: Rep Row 2 of Sleeve Decrease, turn.

Rep Row 2 of csp 3 (5, 1, 1) times, fasten off.

Finishing

BLOCKING AND SEAMING

Pin Back, Fronts (Left and Right), and Sleeves to schematic size. Spritz with water and allow to dry. Pin RS of Fronts and Back together. Seam shoulders by sl st through both fabrics at once. Pin RS of Sleeves and Front/Back panels together. Whipstitch sleeve and side seams together with leftover yarn. Turn right side out.

COLLAR

Join MC at edge of neck on the RS.

Row 1: Ch 1, sc evenly across neck in an odd number of sts, turn.

Row 2: Ch 1, *sc in next sc, ch 1, sk 1 sc, rep from * across to last sc, sc in last sc, turn.

Row 3: Ch 1, sc in first sc, *sc in next ch-1 sp, ch 1, sk 1 sc, rep from * across to last ch-1 sp, sc in last ch-1 sp, sc in last sc, turn.

Row 4: Ch 1, sc in first sc, *ch 1, sk 1 sc, sc in next ch-1 sp, rep from * across to last sc, ch 1, sc in last sc, turn.

Rep Rows 3–4 three times. Rep Row 3 once, fasten off.

EDGING

Join CC at edge of back on the RS.

Row 1: Ch 1, sc evenly across body, 3 sc at edge of body and front panel edge, turn work 90 degrees, sc evenly up Front panel and Collar, 3 sc at edge of Collar, turn work 90 degrees, sc evenly across Collar, 3 sc at edge of opposite Front panel, turn work 90 degrees, sc evenly down Front panel, 3 sc at edge of body, turn work 90 degrees, sc evenly across body to first sc, sl st in first sc, do not turn.

Row 2: Ch 1, rev sc in each sc around entire edge, sl st to first rev sc, fasten off, weave in ends.

FROG CLOSURES

Loop Side (Make 2):

Ch 44 with G/6 (4.25 mm) hook and CC, sl st in ea ch across to end, fasten off leaving a long tail (minimum of 18" [45.5 cm]) for sewing. *Place 2 pins horizontally into a blocking surface, 1½" (3.8 cm) apart in N/S direction*. Place 2 pins horizontally into the blocking surface 2¼" (5.5 cm) apart in E/W direction, creating an even "diamond" shape as shown in **figure 1**. Pin one end of chain in the center of the pins. Loop other end around E (right) pin in a counterclockwise direction (**figure 1**). Loop end around center pin and then around S (bottom) pin in counterclockwise direction. Tuck end under previous loop at center and then loop end around N (top) pin in clockwise direction (**figure 2**). Loop end around center pin and then W (left) pin in clockwise direction. Tuck end under work at center (**figure 3**). Pin center of closure securely together. Remove pins from blocking surface, leaving center securing pins in place on closure. Turn closure over. With tapestry needle, secure center of closure with long tail by stitching through all layers (**figure 7**; make sure your stitches are small enough on the RS of the closure so that they do not show). Weave in opposite end. With tapestry needle and long end, whipstitch loop side of closure to the RS of fabric using photo on page 36 as a general guide.

Button Side (Make 2):

With CC, make adjustable ring, ch 1.

Rnd 1: Sc 4 times in ring, pull ring closed, pm in last st, do not join, working a spiral, moving m up as work progresses, do not turn.

Rnd 2: 2 sc in next sc and in each sc around, do not turn—8 sc.

Rnd 3: Sc in each sc around, do not turn.

Rnd 4: *Sc2tog over next 2 sc, rep from * around, do not turn—4 sc.

Rnd 5: Sc4tog over next 4 sc (button created), ch 35, turn.

Row 6: Sl st in 2nd ch from hook and in each ch back to button, fasten off, leaving long tail (minimum of 18" [45.5 cm]) for sewing.

Squish button flat. Using tapestry needle and long tail, secure button flat by sewing through center multiple times. Repeat instructions from * to * of Loop Side to place N/S (vertical) pins on blocking surface. Place one pin 1⅛" (2.8 cm) to the E (right) of the center. Place one pin in the center. Pin button off center slightly, towards the W (left) direction. Loop end around N (top) pin in counterclockwise direction. Tuck end under ch at center (**figure 4**). Loop end around E (right) pin in counterclockwise direction and over ch at center pin (**figure 5**). Loop end around S (bottom) pin in counterclockwise direction and tuck end under center. Pin end to back of button (**figure 6**). Pin center of closure securely together. Remove pins from blocking surface, leaving securing pins in place on closure. Turn closure over. With tapestry needle, secure center of closure with long tail by stitching through all layers (make sure your stitches are small enough on the RS of the closure so that they do not show; see **figure 7**). Whipstitch button side of closure to the RS of fabric, directly across from corresponding loop side.

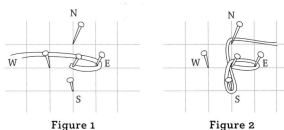

Figure 1   Figure 2

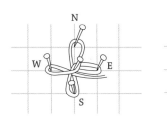

Figure 3   Figure 4

Figure 5   Figure 6

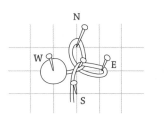

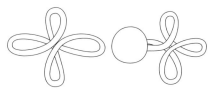

Figure 7

hank
Vest

This vest is for the little boy who is always on the run and for parents who dig style. The vest is constructed with extended single crochet, which will produce a thin fabric that makes the vest easy to wear. The streamlined, contrasting color shapes near the shoulders add just a touch of sophistication to the vest and will keep you occupied as you crochet. The zip-up front makes the vest easy to get on and off, while the washable wool-blend yarn makes it a snap to machine wash.

Equipment

YARN: Worsted weight (#4 Medium).

Shown: Spud and Chloë, Sweater (55% superwash wool, 45% organic cotton; 160 yd [146.3 m]/ 3.5 oz [100 g]): #7504 lake (MC) 2 (2, 3, 3) hanks; #7502 grass (CC) 1 (1, 1, 1) hank.

HOOK: H/8 (5.00 mm) or hook needed to obtain gauge.

NOTIONS: Tapestry needle for weaving in ends; 12 (12, 14, 16)" (30.5 [30.5, 35.5, 40.5] cm) matching molded separating sport zipper; matching sewing thread and hand-sewing needle; spray bottle with water and straight pins for blocking.

Gauge

14 esc by 12 rows = 4" × 4" (10 × 10 cm).

Finished Size

Small (Medium, Large, Extra Large) pullover is sized to fit 6 (12, 18, 24) mths with a relaxed fit. Pullover shown is a size Medium (12 mths).

Finished Chest: 22 (24, 26, 28½)" (56 [61, 66, 72.5] cm).

Finished Length: 11⅜ (12, 14⅝, 15⅜)" (28.8 [30.5, 37.2, 39] cm).

The Plans

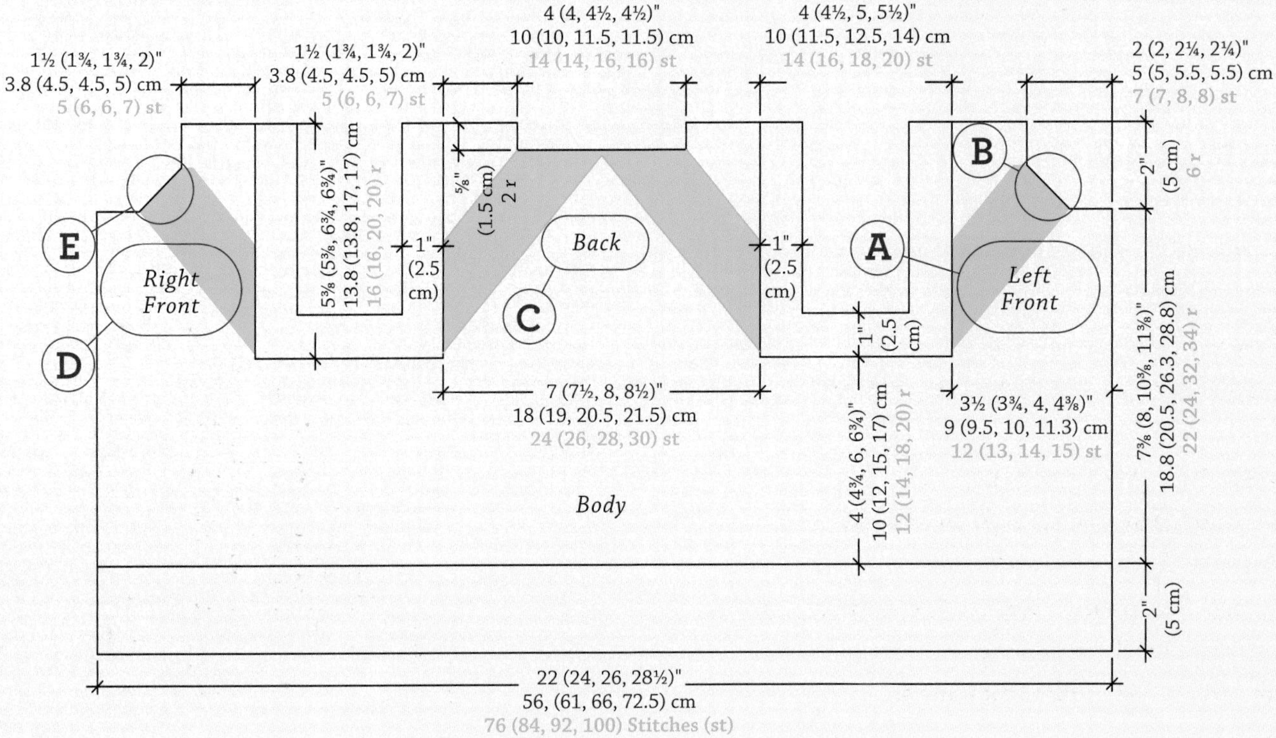
1½ (1¾, 1¾, 2)"
3.8 (4.5, 4.5, 5) cm
5 (6, 6, 7) st
1½ (1¾, 1¾, 2)"
3.8 (4.5, 4.5, 5) cm
5 (6, 6, 7) st
4 (4, 4½, 4½)"
10 (10, 11.5, 11.5) cm
14 (14, 16, 16) st
4 (4½, 5, 5½)"
10 (11.5, 12.5, 14) cm
14 (16, 18, 20) st
2 (2, 2¼, 2¼)"
5 (5, 5.5, 5.5) cm
7 (7, 8, 8) st
B
E
D
A
C
Right Front
Back
Left Front
Body
5⅜ (5⅜, 6¾, 6¾)"
13.8 (13.8, 17, 17) cm
16 (16, 20, 20) r
⅝"
(1.5 cm)
2 r
1"
(2.5 cm)
1"
(2.5 cm)
1"
(2.5 cm)
2"
(5 cm)
6 r
7 (7½, 8, 8½)"
18 (19, 20.5, 21.5) cm
24 (26, 28, 30) st
3½ (3¾, 4, 4⅜)"
9 (9.5, 10, 11.3) cm
12 (13, 14, 15) st
4 (4¾, 6, 6¾)"
10 (12, 15, 17) cm
12 (14, 18, 20) r
7⅜ (8, 10⅜, 11⅜)"
18.8 (20.5, 26.3, 28.8) cm
22 (24, 32, 34) r
2"
(5 cm)
22 (24, 26, 28½)"
56, (61, 66, 72.5) cm
76 (84, 92, 100) Stitches (st)

NOTE: Color changes in stitch diagrams highlight where to change between MC and CC.

Construction

Extended Single Crochet (esc) p. 147

BODY

Ch 77 (85, 93, 101) with MC.

Row 1 (RS): Esc in 3rd ch from hook (sk ch count as esc), esc in ea ch across, turn—76 (84, 92, 100) esc.

Row 2: Ch 2 (counts as esc), esc in ea esc across, turn.
Rep Row 2 ten (twelve, sixteen, eighteen) times.

LEFT FRONT PANEL

See **Stitch Diagram A** at right for assistance.

Change yarns from MC to CC where color on stitch diagram changes from black to aqua, and vice versa, throughout Left Front Panel. Note that color change begins on Row 1 for S and M, and on Row 5 for L and XL.

Row 1: Ch 2 (counts as esc), esc in next 11 (12, 13, 14) esc, turn, leave rem sts unworked—12 (13, 14, 15) esc.
Rep Row 2 of Body 9 (9, 13, 13) times, fasten off.

LEFT NECK

See **Stitch Diagram B** at right for assistance.

Change yarns from MC to CC where color on stitch diagram changes from black to aqua, and vice versa, throughout Left Neck.

Row 1: Sk 3 (3, 4, 4) sts, join yarn with sl st to next esc, sc in next esc, esc in ea esc across to end, turn—7 (8, 8, 9) esc.

Row 2: Ch 2 (counts as esc), esc in ea esc across to last esc, sc in last esc, sl st in sc, turn—6 (7, 7, 8) esc.

Row 3: Sk sl st, sl st in sc, sc in next esc, esc in next esc and ea esc to end, turn—5 (6, 6, 7) esc.
Rep Row 2 of body 3 times, fasten off.

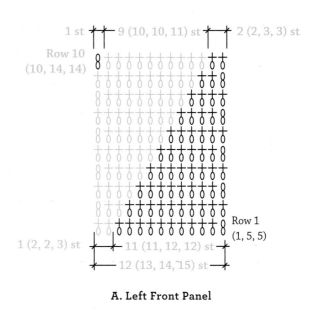

A. Left Front Panel

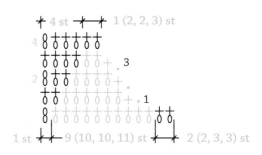

B. Left Neck

BACK

See **Stitch Diagram C** below for assistance.

Change yarns from MC to CC where color on stitch diagram changes from black to aqua, and vice versa, throughout Back. Note that color change begins on Row 1 for S and M, and on Row 5 for L and XL.

Row 1: Sk 14 (16, 18, 20) sts from end of Row 1 of Left Front Panel, join yarn to next esc with sl st, ch 2 (counts as esc), esc in next 23 (25, 27, 29) esc, turn, leave rem sts unworked—24 (26, 28, 30) esc.

Rep Row 2 of Body 13 (13, 17, 17) times.

SHOULDERS

Row 1a: Ch 2 (counts as esc), esc in next 4 (5, 5, 5) esc, turn, leave rem sts unworked—5 (6, 6, 7) esc.

Rep Row 2 of Body once, fasten off.

Row 1b: Sk 14 (14, 16, 16) sts from end of Row 1a, join yarn to next esc with sl st, ch 2 (counts as esc), esc in ea esc across to end, turn—5 (6, 6, 7) esc.

Rep Row 2 of Body once, fasten off.

RIGHT FRONT PANEL

See **Stitch Diagram D** below for assistance.

Change yarns from MC to CC where color on stitch diagram changes from black to aqua, and vice versa, throughout Right Front Panel. Note that color change begins on Row 1 for S and M, and on Row 5 for L and XL.

Row 1: Sk 14 (16, 18, 20) sts from end of Row 1 of Back panel, join yarn to next esc with sl st, ch 2 (counts as esc), esc in ea esc to end, turn—12 (13, 14, 15) esc.

Rep Row 2 of Body 9 (9, 13, 13) times, turn.

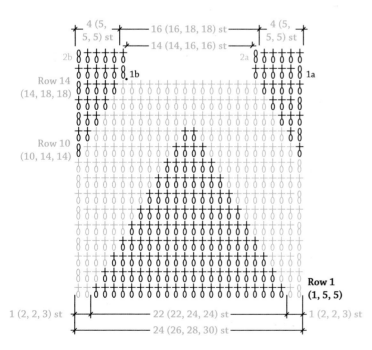

C. Back Panel

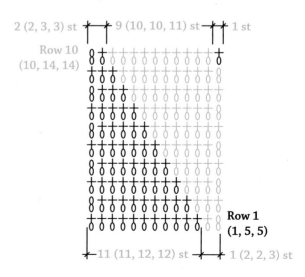

D. Right Front Panel

RIGHT NECK

See **Stitch Diagram E** below for assistance.

Change yarns from MC to CC where color on stitch diagram changes from black to aqua, and vice versa, throughout neck.

Row 1: Ch 2 (counts as esc), esc in next 6 (7, 7, 8) esc, sc in next esc, sl st in next esc, turn, leave rem sts unworked— 7 (8, 8, 9) esc.

Row 2: Sk sl st, sl st in sc, sc in next esc, esc in next esc and ea esc to end, turn—6 (7, 7, 8) esc.

Row 3: Ch 2 (counts as esc), esc in ea esc across to last esc, sc in last esc, sl st in sc, turn—5 (6, 6, 7) esc.

Row 4: Sk sl st, sl st in sc, sl st in first esc, ch 2 (counts as esc), esc in ea esc to end, turn.

Rep Row 2 of Body twice, fasten off.

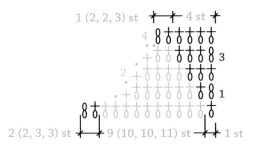

E. Right Neck

Finishing

BLOCKING, SEAMING & EMBROIDERY

Pin body to schematic size. Spritz with water and allow to dry. Pin RS of front and back together. Seam shoulders by sl st through both fabrics at once. Turn right side out. Following lines of color work, sl st on top of fabric to accentuate the diagonal line with CC. Join MC to edge of Front Panel with sl st, ch 1, sc evenly up edge to straighten out row ends, fasten off, weave in ends.

BOTTOM RIBBING

Join MC with sl st to bottom edge, ch 10.

Row 1: Sc in 2nd ch from hook and each ch across, sl st in next 2 sts of Body twice (first sl st joins ribbing to body, second counts as a tch), turn—9 sc.

Row 2: Sc-blp in each sc across, turn.

Row 3: Ch 1, sc-blp in ea sc across, sl st in next 2 sts of Body, turn.

Rep Rows 2–3 evenly around Body, omitting last 2 sl sts, fasten off, weave in ends.

COLLAR

Join MC with sl st to neck edge, ch 10. Follow directions for Bottom Ribbing around neck—10 sc.

ARMHOLE RIBBING

Join MC with sl st to underarm, ch 6. Follow directions for Bottom Ribbing around armhole—5 sc. With tapestry needle, whipstitch first and last rows together.

ZIPPER

Pin zipper to Front Panels. With backstitch, matching thread, and handsewing needle, sew zipper to panels securely.

leah
Pullover

After shopping for clothes for my daughter, I was surprised at the lack of sweaters for babies. Unfortunately, even when there were sweaters available, they were certainly not something I would want to dress her in. That inspired me to whip up this tunic sweater, which is so adorable I am thinking of making one for myself. It is crocheted from the neck down, so you can try it on your model as you go, making the project fun for both of you.

Equipment

YARN: DK weight (#3 Light).

Shown: Naturally Caron, Country (75% microdenier acrylic, 25% merino wool; 185 yd [170 m]/ 3 oz [85 g]): #0014 deep purple (MC), 2 (3, 3, 4) hanks; #0004 green sheen (CC), 1 (1, 1, 1) hank.

HOOK: H/8 (5.00 mm) or hook needed to obtain gauge.

NOTIONS: Tapestry needle for weaving in ends; 3 stitch markers; spray bottle with water and straight pins for blocking; three ⅝" (1.5 cm) buttons; 3 size 2 snaps; 12" (30.5 cm) of ½" (1.3 cm) wide grosgrain ribbon; hand-sewing needle and thread.

Gauge

3 sh (3 SR) by 12 rows (6 RR)= 4⅞" × 4⅞" (12.4 × 12.4 cm) in Bonny Stitch Pattern (bsp).

Finished Size

Small (Medium, Large, Extra Large) sweater is sized to fit 6 (12, 18, 24) mths with a relaxed fit. Sweater shown is a size Extra Large (24 mths).

Finished Chest: 21 (22¾, 24½, 26)" (53.5 [58, 62, 66] cm).

Finished Length: 12⅜ (13¼, 15⅝, 16½)" (31.3 [33.5, 39.8, 42] cm).

The Plans

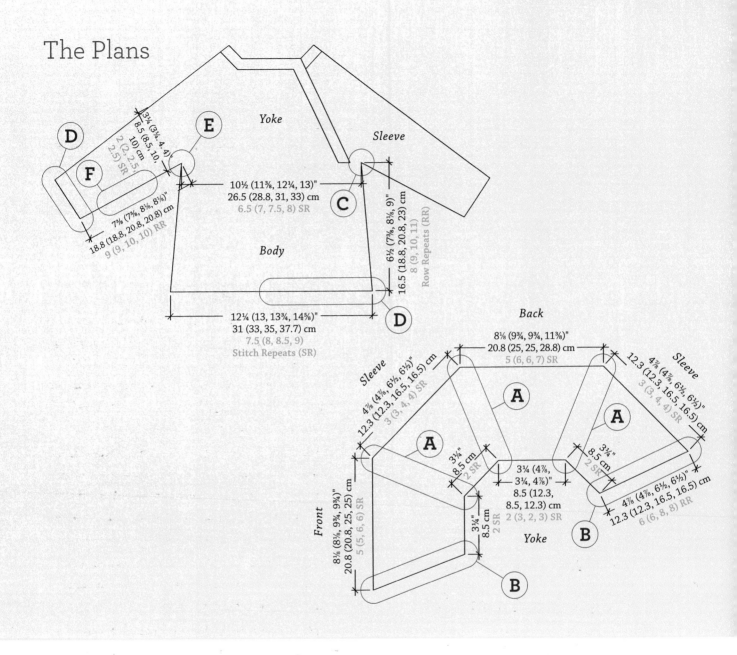

Yoke

Sleeve

3¾ (3¾, 4, 4)
8.5 (8.5, 10,
10) cm
2 (2, 2.5,
2.5) SR

D

E

F

10½ (11⅜, 12¼, 13)"
26.5 (28.8, 31, 33) cm
6.5 (7, 7.5, 8) SR

C

7⅜ (7⅜, 8⅛, 8⅛)"
18.8 (18.8, 20.8, 20.8) cm
9 (9, 10, 10) RR

6½ (7⅜, 8⅛, 9)"
16.5 (18.8, 20.8, 23) cm
8 (9, 10, 11)
Row Repeats (RR)

Body

D

12¼ (13, 13¾, 14⅝)"
31 (33, 35, 37.7) cm
7.5 (8, 8.5, 9)
Stitch Repeats (SR)

Sleeve

Back

Sleeve

8⅛ (9¾, 9¾, 11⅜)"
20.8 (25, 25, 28.8) cm
5 (6, 6, 7) SR

4⅞ (4⅞, 6½, 6½)"
12.3 (12.3, 16.5, 16.5) cm
3 (3, 4, 4) SR

A

4⅞ (4⅞, 6½, 6½)"
12.3 (12.3, 16.5, 16.5) cm
3 (3, 4, 4) SR

A

A

3¼"
8.5 cm
2 SR

3¼ (4⅞,
3¼, 4⅞)"
8.5 (12.3,
8.5, 12.3) cm
2 (3, 2, 3) SR

3¼"
8.5 cm
2 SR

4⅞ (4⅞, 6½, 6½)"
12.3 (12.3, 16.5, 16.5) cm
6 (6, 8, 8) RR

B

Front

8⅛ (8⅛, 9¾, 9¾)"
20.8 (20.8, 25, 25) cm
5 (5, 6, 6) SR

3¼"
8.5 cm
2 SR

Yoke

B

NOTE: Stitch pattern is reversible.

Details

SHELL (SH)

(2 dc, ch 2, 2 dc) in st indicated.

BONNY STITCH PATTERN (BSP)

See **Bonny Stitch Pattern** diagram below for assistance.

Ch 28.

Row 1: 2 dc in 4th ch from hook, *sk 3 ch, (sc, ch 3, sc) in next ch, sk 3 ch, sh in next ch, rep from * across to last 8 ch, sk 3 ch, (sc, ch 3, sc) in next ch, sk 3 ch, 3 dc in last ch, turn—2 sh, 3 SR.

Row 2: Ch 3 (counts as hdc, ch 1), sc in first dc, *sh in next ch-3 sp, (sc, ch 3, sc) in next ch-2 sp, rep from * across to last ch-3 sp, sh in last ch-3 sp, (sc, ch 1, hdc) in top of tch, turn—3 sh, 3 SR.

Row 3: Ch 3 (counts as dc), 2 dc in first hdc, (sc, ch 3, sc) in next ch-2 sp, *sh in next ch-3 sp, (sc, ch 3, sc) in next ch-2 sp, rep from * across to last ch-2 sp, 3 dc in 2nd ch of tch, turn—2 sh, 3 SR.

Rep Rows 2–3 for pattern.

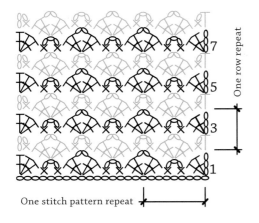

One row repeat

One stitch pattern repeat

Bonny Stitch Pattern (bsp)

Construction

YOKE

With MC, ch 68 (76, 68, 76).

Row 1: Dc in 4th ch from hook, *sk 3 ch, (sc, ch 3, sc) in next ch, sk 3 ch, sh in next ch, rep from * across to last 8 sk, sk 3 ch, (sc, ch 3, sc) in next ch, sk 3 ch, 3 dc in last ch, turn—7 (8, 7, 8) sh, 8 (9, 8, 9) SR.

Rep Row 2 of bsp across once before cont—8 (9, 8, 9) sh, 8 (9, 8, 9) SR.

Yoke Increase:

See **Stitch Diagrams A and B** on page 54 for assistance.

Row 1: Ch 5 (counts as dc, ch 2), 2 dc in first hdc, cont in bsp for 2 ch-2 sps, (2 dc, ch 2, 2 dc, ch 2, 2 dc) in next ch-3 sp (inc made), pm in 2nd 2-dc group, cont in bsp for 2, (3, 2, 3) ch-2 sps, inc in next ch-3 sp, pm, cont in bsp for 2 ch-2 sps, inc in next ch-3 sp, pm, cont in bsp across to end, (2 dc, ch 2, dc) in 2nd ch of tch, turn.

Row 2: Ch 2 (counts as hdc), (sc, ch 3, sc) in next ch-2 sp, *cont in bsp across to sp before m, (sc, ch 3, sc) in next ch-2 sp, hdc bet middle 2-dc group, pm in hdc, (sc, ch 3, sc) in next ch-2 sp, (inc made), rep from * across, cont in bsp across to end, (sc, ch 3, sc) in ch-sp, hdc in 3rd ch of tch, turn.

Row 3: Ch 3 (counts as dc), *cont in bsp across to m, (sc, ch 3, sc) in hdc (inc made), rep from * across, cont in bsp across to end, dc in top of tch, turn.

Row 4: Ch 3 (counts as dc), 2 dc in first dc, cont in bsp across to end, 3 dc in top of tch, turn—11 (12, 11, 12) sh + 2 half sh; 12 (13, 12, 13) SR.

Row 5: Ch 1, (sc, ch 3, sc) in first dc, cont in bsp for 2 ch-2 sps, (2 dc, ch 2, 2 dc, ch 2, 2 dc) in next ch-3 sp (inc made), pm in 2nd 2-dc group, cont in bsp for 4, (5, 4, 5) ch-2 sps, inc in next ch-3 sp, pm, cont in bsp for 2 ch-2 sps, inc in next ch-3 sp, pm, cont in bsp across to end, (sc, ch 3, sc) in top of tch, turn.

Row 6: Ch 3 (counts as dc), (dc, ch 2, 2 dc) in next ch-3 sp, (sc, ch 3, sc) in next ch-2 sp, *cont in bsp across to m, (sc, ch 3, sc) in next ch-2 sp, hdc bet middle 2-dc group, pm in hdc, (sc, ch 3, sc) in next ch-2 sp, (inc made), rep from * across, cont in bsp across to last ch-3 sp, (2dc, ch 2, dc) in last ch-3 sp, dc in last sc, turn—13 (14, 13, 14) sh, 13 (14, 13, 14) SR.

Row 7: Ch 4 (counts as dc, ch 1), *cont in bsp across to m, (sc, ch 3, sc) in hdc (inc made), rep from * across, cont in bsp across to end, ch 1, dc in top of tch, turn—15 (16, 15, 16) sh, 15 (16, 15, 16) SR.

Row 8: Ch 3 (counts as hdc, ch 1), sc in first dc, cont in bsp across to end, (sc, ch 1, hdc) in 3rd ch of tch, turn—16 (17, 16, 17) sh, 16 (17, 16, 17) SR.

(L/XL only) Row 9: Ch 5 (counts as dc, ch 2), 2 dc in hdc, cont in bsp for 3 ch-2 sps, (2 dc, ch 2, 2 dc, ch 2, 2 dc) in next ch-3 sp (inc made), pm in 2nd 2-dc group, cont in bsp for 5 (6) ch-2 sps, inc in next ch-3 sp, pm, cont in bsp for 3 ch-2 sps, inc in next ch-3 sp, pm, cont in bsp across to end, (2 dc, ch 2, dc) in 2nd ch of tch, turn.

Rep Rows 2–4 once—19 (20) sh + 2 half sh; 20 (21) SR.

(All) Last Row: Ch 1, turn work 90 degrees, sc evenly up edge (ends of rows) to neck edge, 2 sc in first foundation ch of neck edge, turn work 90 degrees, 3 sc in ea ch-sp across to last ch, 2 sc in last ch of neck edge, turn work 90 degrees, sc evenly down edge, turn, fasten off MC.

A. Yoke Increase

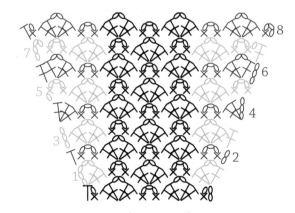

B. Yoke Row Ends

FIRST RAGLAN TRIM

With WS facing, join CC to last sc on edge of Yoke.

Row 1 (WS): Ch 1, sc in ea sc across, turn.

Rep Row 1 three times, fasten off.

SECOND RAGLAN TRIM

With WS facing, join CC at corner of neck edge on opposite side edge. Rep First Raglan Trim on opposite side edge, fasten off.

COLLAR

With WS facing, join CC to corner of neck edge with sl st.

Row 1 (WS): Ch 1, sc evenly across collar and ends of raglan trims, turn.

Row 2: Ch 1, sc in ea sc across, turn.

Rep Row 2 twice, fasten off.

JOINING FOR BODY

Pin raglan seams together by placing the right side on top of the left side. With WS facing, join MC to 3rd ch-3 sp (3rd ch-3 sp, 4th sh, 4th sh) from end of last row of Yoke with sl st. See **Stitch Diagram C** at right for assistance.

(S/M) Rnd 1: Ch 3, 2 dc in same ch-sp, cont in bsp for 5 (6) sh, 3 dc in next ch-3 sp, ch 7, sk next 2 sh, 3 dc in next ch-3 sp, cont bsp across, 5 sc across raglan ends evenly, 3 dc in t-ch, ch 7, sk remaining sh, sl st to 3rd ch of tch, turn.

(S/M) Rnd 2: Ch 1, sc in top of t-ch, sk 3 ch, sh in next ch, sk 3 ch, (sc, ch 3, sc) in next dc, sk 2 sc, sh in next sc, sk 2 sc, (sc, ch 3, sc) in next dc, cont in bsp to ch-7 sp, (sc, ch 3, sc) in last dc, sk 3 ch, sh in next ch, sk 3 ch, (sc, ch 3, sc) in next dc, cont in bsp across to end, sc in top of t-ch, ch 1, hdc in first sc, turn—13 (14) sh or SR.

(L/XL) Rnd 1: Ch 3, sc in same ch-sp, cont in bsp for 6 (7) sh, (sc, ch 1, hdc) in next ch-2 sp, ch 7, sk next 3 ch-3 sps, (hdc,

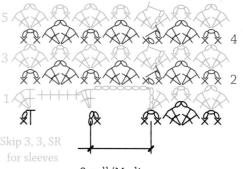

Skip 3, 3, SR for sleeves

Small/Medium

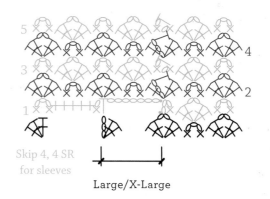

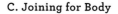

Skip 4, 4 SR for sleeves

Large/X-Large

C. Joining for Body

ch 1, sc) in next ch-2 sp, cont bsp across, (sc, ch 3, sc) in last dc, 5 sc across raglan ends evenly, (sc, ch 1, hdc) in first dc, ch 7, sk remaining ch-3 sps, sl st to 2nd ch of tch, turn.

(L/XL) Rnd 2: Ch 3 (counts as dc), dc in 2nd ch of t-ch, sk 3 ch, (sc, ch 3, sc) in next ch, sk 3 ch, sh in next hdc, sk 2 sc, (sc, ch 3, sc) in next sc, sk 2 sc, cont in bsp across to ch-7 sp, sh in hdc, sk 3 ch, (sc, ch 3, sc) in next ch, sk 3 ch, sh in next hdc, cont in bsp across to end, 2 dc in same ch as first dc, hdc in top of tch, turn—(15, 16) sh or SR.

(L/XL) Rnd 3: Ch 1, sc around hdc, cont in bsp across to end, sc around hdc, ch 1, hdc in first sc, turn.

BODY INCREASE

Rnd 1: Ch 3 (counts as dc), dc around hdc, cont in bsp across to end, 2 dc around hdc, hdc in top of tch, turn.

Rnd 2: Ch 1, sc around hdc, cont in bsp across to end, sc around hdc, ch 1, hdc in first sc, turn.

Rnd 3: Ch 3 (counts as dc), dc around hdc, cont in bsp across for 6 (7, 7, 8) sh, (2 dc, ch 2, 2 dc, ch 2, 2 dc) in next ch-3 sp, pm in 2nd 2-dc group, cont in bsp across to end, (2 dc, ch 2, 2 dc) around hdc, hdc in top of tch, turn.

Rnd 4: Ch 1, sc around hdc, hdc bet next 2 dc, (sc, ch 3, sc) in next ch-2 sp, cont in bsp across to m, hdc bet dc group, pm in hdc, (sc, ch 3, sc) in next ch-2 sp, cont in bsp across to end, sc around hdc, ch 1, hdc in first sc, turn.

Rnd 5: Ch 3 (counts as dc), dc around hdc, cont in bsp across to m, (sc, ch 3, sc) in hdc, cont in bsp across to next hdc, (sc, ch 3, sc) in next hdc, 2 dc around post of first hdc, hdc in top of tch, turn—15 (16, 17, 18) sh or SR.
Rep Rnd 2 once. Rep Rnds 1–2 four (five, five, six) times.

(L/XL only) Rep Rnd 1 once.

EDGING

See **Stitch Diagram D** below for assistance.

Rnd 1: Ch 1, sc in hdc, *ch 2, 2 sc in next ch-sp, ch 2, 2 sc in next ch-sp, rep from * across, ch 2, 2 sc in next ch-sp, ch 2, sc around post of hdc, sl st in first sc, turn.

Rnd 2: Ch 1, sc in ea sc and 2 sc in ea ch-2 sp around, sl st in first sc, fasten off.

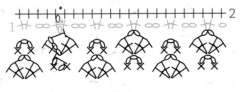

D. Edging

SLEEVE

Join MC to WS edge of sleeve at edge of chain with sl st around post of hdc (hdc, dc, dc). See **Stitch Diagrams E and F** below and on page 57 for assistance.

Joining Sleeves:

(S/M) Rnd 1: Ch 3, dc around post of dc, (sc, ch 3, sc) in next ch-2 sp, cont in bsp around to chain, sh around post of dc (or tch from prev join), sk 3 ch, (sc, ch 3, sc) in next ch, sk 3 ch, 2 dc around post of dc, hdc in top of t-ch, turn—4 (4) sh or SR.

(L/XL) Rnd 1: Ch 1, sc around post of hdc, sh in next ch-3 sp, cont in bsp around to chain, (sc, ch 3, sc) around post of hdc (or tch from prev join), sk 3 ch, sh in next ch, sk 3 ch, sc around post of hdc, ch 1, hdc in first sc, turn—(5, 5) sh or SR.

(L/XL) Rnd 2: Ch 3 (counts as dc), dc around hdc, cont in bsp across to end, 2 dc around hdc, hdc in top of tch, turn.

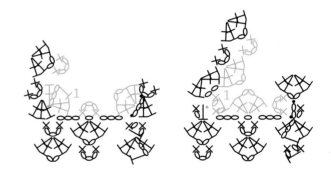

E. Joining Sleeves

Sleeves:

Rnd 1: Ch 1, sc around hdc, cont in bsp across to end, sc around hdc, ch 1, hdc in first sc, turn.

Rnd 2: Ch 3 (counts as dc), dc around hdc, cont in bsp across to end, 2 dc around hdc, hdc in top of tch, turn.

Rep Rnds 1–2 seven (seven, eight, eight) times, (S/M only) Rep Rnd 1 once.

Cont with 2 Body Edging Rnds, fasten off.

F. Working in Rounds

Finishing

BLOCKING AND BUTTONS

Pin to schematic size (see The Plans on page 52). Spritz with water and allow to dry. With first button 2" (5 cm) below top edge and last button 1½" (4 cm) above bottom edge of trim, sew 3 buttons, evenly spaced, across front trim. Cut the grosgrain ribbon in half. Then, using the thread and handsewing needle, sew one half of each snap to each piece of ribbon securely, centering the snaps and leaving the same gap between the snaps as you left between the buttons. Sew the grosgrain ribbon to the inside of the collar, corresponding to the placement of the buttons. Be sure to fold under the short edges of the grosgrain ribbon as you stitch it down to hide the raw edges.

charlie
Vest

This vest brings back memories of watching that popular children's show, *Mister Rogers' Neighborhood*. The lead character, the beloved Mr. Rogers, always wore classic zip-up sweaters. The retro style of this little boy's vest, mixed with a tweed stitch pattern, is reminiscent of those classic cardigans. If you are in the mood to update the style, try using a bold, vivid color for the main yarn and let the contrasting yarn be in a subtle, complementary color.

Equipment

YARN: Worsted weight (#4 Medium). *Shown:* Spud and Chloë, Sweater (55% superwash wool, 45% organic cotton; 160 yd [146.3 m]/3.5 oz [100 g]): #7506 toast (MC) 1 (1, 2, 2) hanks; #7511 chipmunk (CC) 1 (1, 1, 1) hank.

HOOK: H/8 (5.00 mm) or hook needed to obtain gauge.

NOTIONS: Tapestry needle for weaving in ends; 6 (6, 8, 8)" (15 [15, 20.5, 20.5] cm) matching molded separating sport zipper; matching sewing thread and handsewing needle; spray bottle with water and straight pins for blocking.

Gauge

18 sts by 10 rows (9 SR and 2 ½ RR) = 4" × 3¾" (10 × 9.5 cm) in Tweed Stitch Pattern (tsp).

Finished Size

Small (Medium, Large, Extra Large) vest is sized to fit 6 (12, 18, 24) mths with a relaxed fit. Vest shown is a size Extra Large (24 mths).

Finished chest: 21 (23, 24½, 26½)" (53.5 [58.5, 62, 67.5] cm).

Finished length: 11¼ (11¼, 14¼, 14¼)" (28.5 [28.5, 36, 36] cm).

The Plans

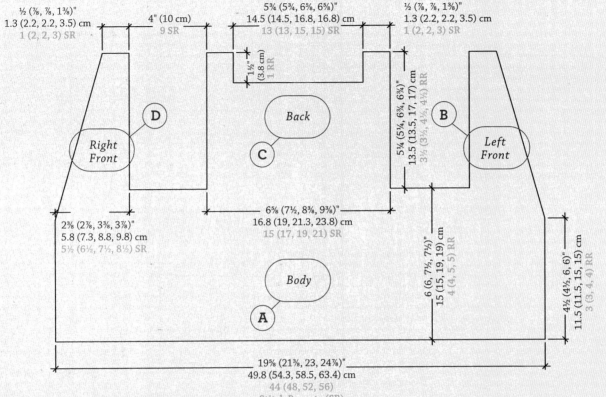

½ (⅞, ⅞, 1⅜)"
1.3 (2.2, 2.2, 3.5) cm
1 (2, 2, 3) SR

4" (10 cm)
9 SR

5¾ (5¾, 6⅝, 6⅝)"
14.5 (14.5, 16.8, 16.8) cm
13 (13, 15, 15) SR

½ (⅞, ⅞, 1⅜)"
1.3 (2.2, 2.2, 3.5) cm
1 (2, 2, 3) SR

1½" (3.8 cm)
1 RR

D

Right Front

Back

C

B

Left Front

5¼ (5¾, 6¾, 6¾)"
13.5 (13.5, 17, 17) cm
3½ (3½, 4½, 4½) RR

2⅜ (2⅞, 3⅜, 3⅞)"
5.8 (7.3, 8.8, 9.8) cm
5½ (6½, 7½, 8½) SR

6⅝ (7½, 8⅜, 9⅜)"
16.8 (19, 21.3, 23.8) cm
15 (17, 19, 21) SR

Body

A

6 (6, 7½, 7½)"
15 (15, 19, 19) cm
4 (4, 5, 5) RR

4½ (4½, 6, 6)"
11.5 (11.5, 15, 15) cm
3 (3, 4, 4) RR

19⅝ (21⅜, 23, 24⅞)"
49.8 (54.3, 58.5, 63.4) cm
44 (48, 52, 56)
Stitch Repeats (SR)

12
10
8
6
4
2

11
9
7
5
3
1

One row repeat

One stitch pattern repeat

Tweed Stitch Pattern (tsp)

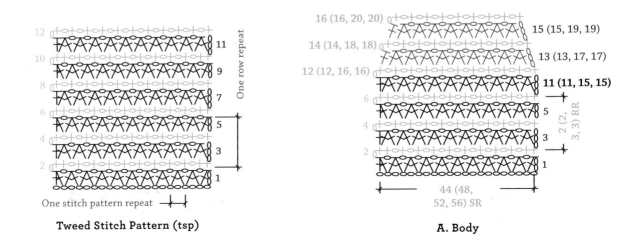

16 (16, 20, 20)
14 (14, 18, 18)
12 (12, 16, 16)

6
4
2

15 (15, 19, 19)
13 (13, 17, 17)
11 (11, 15, 15)

5
3
1

2 (2, 3, 3) RR

44 (48, 52, 56) SR

A. Body

NOTE: Change yarn colors between MC and CC after each row. Leave a 1½" (3.8 cm) tail at the end of each row. Tails will be hidden with edging.

Details

TWEED STITCH PATTERN (TSP)

See **Tweed Stitch Pattern** diagram on page 60 for assistance.

Ch 23 with MC.

Row 1(RS): Dc in 4th ch from hook, *ch 1, dc2tog in same ch and 2 ch away (sk one ch), rep from * across to last 2 ch, ch 1, dc2tog in last 2 ch, turn, fasten off MC—10 dc2tog.

Row 2: Join CC, ch 1, sc in dc2tog, *sc in ch-1 sp, ch 1, sk dc2tog, rep from * across to last ch-1 sp, sc in last ch-1 sp, sc in dc, turn, fasten off CC.

Row 3: Join MC, ch 3 (counts as dc), dc2tog in first sc and next ch-1 sp, *ch 1, dc2tog in same ch-1 sp and next ch-1 sp, rep from * across to last ch-1 sp, ch 1, dc2tog in last ch-1 sp and last sc, dc in last sc, turn, fasten off MC.

Row 4: Join CC, ch 1, sc in dc, *ch 1, sk dc2tog, sc in ch-1 sp, rep from * across to last ch-1 sp, ch 1, sk dc2tog, sc in top of t-ch, turn, fasten off CC.

Row 5: Join MC, ch 2, dc in ch-1 sp, *ch 1, dc2tog in same ch-1 sp and next ch-1 sp, rep from * across to last ch-1 sp, ch 1, dc2tog in last ch-1 sp and last sc, turn, fasten off MC.

Rep Rows 2–5 for pattern.

Construction

BODY

See **Stitch Diagram A** on page 60 for assistance.

Ch 91 (99, 107, 115) with MC.

Cont in tsp for 12 (12, 16, 16) rows, changing colors after each row—44 (48, 52, 56) dc2tog or SR.

Row 13 (13, 17, 17): Join MC, ch 3, dc2tog in first ch-1 sp and next ch-1 sp, ch 1, cont in tsp across to last ch-1 sp, dc in last sc, turn, fasten off MC.

Row 14 (14, 18, 18): Join CC, ch 1, sc in dc, ch 1, sk dc2tog, cont in tsp across to last ch-1 sp, sc in last ch-1 sp, ch 1, sk last dc2tog, sc in top of tch, turn, fasten off CC—43 (47, 51, 55) ch-1 sps or SR.

Rep prev 2 rows once—42 (46, 50, 54) ch-1 sps or SR.

LEFT FRONT PANEL

See **Stitch Diagram B** below for assistance.

Row 1: Join MC, ch 3, dc2tog in first ch-1 sp and next ch-1 sp, ch 1, cont in tsp across for 4 (5, 6, 7) dc2tog total, dc in same ch-1 sp, turn, leave rem sts unworked, fasten off MC.

Row 2: Join CC, ch 1, sc in dc, ch 1, sk dc2tog, cont in tsp across to last ch-1 sp, sc in last ch-1 sp, ch 1, sk last dc2tog, sc in top of tch, turn, fasten off CC—4 (5, 6, 7) ch-1 sps or SR.

Row 3: Join MC, ch 3, dc2tog in first ch-1 sp and next ch-1 sp, ch 1, cont in tsp across to last ch-1 sp, dc2tog in last ch-1 sp and last sc, turn, fasten off MC.

Row 4: Join CC, ch 1, sc in dc, sc in ch-1 sp, cont in tsp across to last ch-1 sp, sc in last ch-1 sp, ch 1, sk last dc2tog, sc in top of tch, turn, fasten off CC—3 (4, 5, 6) ch-1 sps or SR.

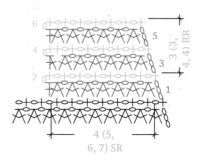

B. Left Front Panel

Row 5: Join MC, ch 3, dc2tog in first ch-1 sp and next ch-1 sp, ch 1, cont in tsp across to last ch-1 sp, dc2tog in last ch-1 sp and last sc, dc in last sc, turn, fasten off MC—3 (4, 5, 6) dc2tog or SR.

Rep Rows 2–5 two (two, three, three) times. Rep Row 2 once.

BACK

See **Stitch Diagram C** below for assistance.

Row 1: Join MC with sl st to 9th ch-1 sp from Left Front Panel, ch 3, dc2tog in same ch-1 sp and next ch-1 sp, ch 1, cont in tsp across for 15 (17, 19, 21) dc2tog total, dc in same ch-1 sp, turn, leave rem sts unworked, fasten off MC.

Cont in tsp for 10 (10, 14, 14) rows total.

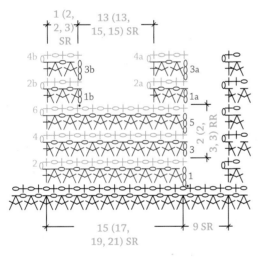

C. Back Panel

SHOULDER

Row 1a: (All sizes) Join MC, ch 2, dc in next ch-1 sp, **(M, L, XL only)** *ch 1, dc2tog in same ch-1 sp and next ch-1 sp, **(XL size only)** rep from * once, **(All sizes)** ch 1, dc2tog in same ch-1 sp and next sc, turn, fasten off MC—1 (2, 2, 3) dc2tog or SR.

Cont in tsp for 3 more rows, fasten off.

Row 1b: (All sizes) Join MC with sl st 13 (13, 15, 15) ch-1 sps from end of Row 1a, ch 2, dc in ch-1 sp, **(M, L, XL only)** *ch 1, dc2tog in same ch-1 sp and next ch-1 sp, **(XL size only)** rep from * once, **(All sizes)** ch 1, dc2tog in same ch-1 sp and last sc, turn, fasten off MC—1 (2, 2, 3) dc2tog or SR.

Cont in tsp for 3 more rows fasten off.

RIGHT FRONT PANEL

See **Stitch Diagram D** below for assistance.

Row 1: Join MC with sl st, 9 ch-1 sps from Back panel, ch 3, dc2tog in first ch-1 sp and next ch-1 sp, ch 1, cont in tsp to last ch-1 sp, dc in last sc, turn, fasten off MC—4 (5, 6, 7) dc2tog or SR.

Row 2: Join CC, ch 1, sc in dc, ch 1, sk dc2tog, cont in tsp across to last ch-1 sp, sc in last ch-1 sp, ch 1, sk last dc2tog, sc in top of tch, turn, fasten off CC—4 (5, 6, 7) ch-1 sps or SR.

Row 3: Join MC, ch 2, dc in first ch-1 sp, ch 1, cont in tsp across to last ch-1 sp, dc in last sc, turn, fasten off MC.

Row 4: Join CC, ch 1, sc in dc, ch 1, sk dc2tog, cont in tsp across to last ch-1 sp, sc in last ch-1 sp, sc in dc, turn, fasten off CC—3 (4, 5, 6) ch-1 sps or SR.

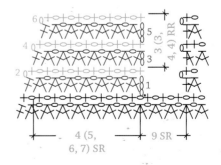

D. Right Front Panel

Row 5: Join MC, ch 3, dc2tog in first sc and next ch-1 sp, ch 1, cont in tsp to last ch-1 sp, dc in last sc, turn, fasten off MC—3 (4, 5, 6) dc2tog or SR.

Rep Rows 2–5 two (two, three, three) times. Rep Row 2 once.

Finishing

BLOCKING AND SEAMING

Pin body to schematic size. Spritz with water and allow to dry. Fold body in half. With RS facing, sl st shoulder seam by working through both Front and Back at once. Turn right side out.

BOTTOM EDGING

Join MC with sl st to RS bottom edge of body, ch 1, sc evenly across bottom, fasten off.

SLEEVE EDGING

Join CC to RS of arm opening.

Rnd 1: Ch 1, sc evenly around arm opening (working over tail ends of MC and CC), sl st to first sc, turn.

Rnd 2: Ch 1, sc in ea sc around, skipping 2 sc at inside corners, sl st to first sc, turn.

Rep Rnd 2 once, fasten off, weave in ends.

NECK EDGING

Join CC to RS of body opening at bottom corner of Front Panel.

Row 1: Ch 1, sc evenly around body and neck opening (working over tail ends of MC and CC), turn.

Row 2: Ch 1, sc in ea sc around, skipping 2 sc at inside corners, 2 sc at outside corners, sl st to first sc, turn.

Rep Row 2 once, fasten off, weave in ends.

Join MC with sl st to bottom of edging at top of Row 1, working through fabric, sl st around neck edging, fasten off, weave in ends.

POCKETS (MAKE 2)

With CC, ch 13.

Row 1: Sc in 2nd ch from hook, sc in ea ch across, turn—12 sc.

Row 2: Ch 1, sc in ea sc across, turn.

Rep Row 2 once.

Rnd 4: Sl st in ea sc across, turn work 90 degrees, sl st down edge of pocket, turn work 90 degrees, sl st in ea ch across, turn work 90 degrees, sl st up edge of pocket, fasten off.

Join MC with sl st to top of pocket across top of Row 2, working on top of fabric, sl st across pocket, fasten off. Using long tail and referring to the photo on page 58 for placement, sew pockets to front panels of vest 1" (2.5 cm) above bottom edge and 1½" (3.8 cm) from front edge.

ZIPPER

Pin zipper to body opening, matching the end of the zipper to the bottom of the body. Fold ends of zipper under so the raw edge won't show. With handsewing needle and thread, use a backstitch to sew zipper to vest securely.

rosa
Car Coat

Just like you, babies enjoy having soft, warm sweaters surrounding them in the cold winter months. This classic car coat will keep your little one warm, but it is crocheted with a lightweight yarn to reduce extra bulk, making it appropriate for fall and spring as well. The granny square collar and cuffs are great for little fingers to caress when they need a little comfort. This adorable sweater will instantly dress up a casual outfit in addition to keeping your sweetie comfortably warm.

Equipment

YARN: *Shown:* Naturally Caron, Spa (75% microdenier acrylic, 25% bamboo; 251 yd [229.5 m]/ 3 oz [85 g]): #0001 rose bisque (MC), 3 (3, 4, 4) balls; #0003 soft sunshine (CC1), 1 (1, 1, 1) ball; #0008 misty taupe (CC2), 1 (1, 1, 1) ball.

HOOK: G/6 (4.00 mm) or hook needed to obtain gauge; G/7 (4.50 mm) hook also needed for S and M sizes.

NOTIONS: Tapestry needle for weaving in ends; 1¼" (32 mm) button; spray bottle with water and straight pins for blocking.

Gauge

28 sts by 16 rows (14 SR and 4 RR) = 6" × 6¼" (15 × 16 cm) in cluster stitch pattern (csp).

Finished Size

Small (Medium, Large, Extra Large) coat is sized to fit 6 (12, 18, 24) mths with a relaxed fit. Coat shown is a size Extra Large (24 mths).

Finished chest: 22 (24, 26, 28)" (56 [61, 66, 71] cm).

Finished length: 12¾ (14, 15¾, 17¼)" (32 [35.5, 40, 44] cm).

The Plans

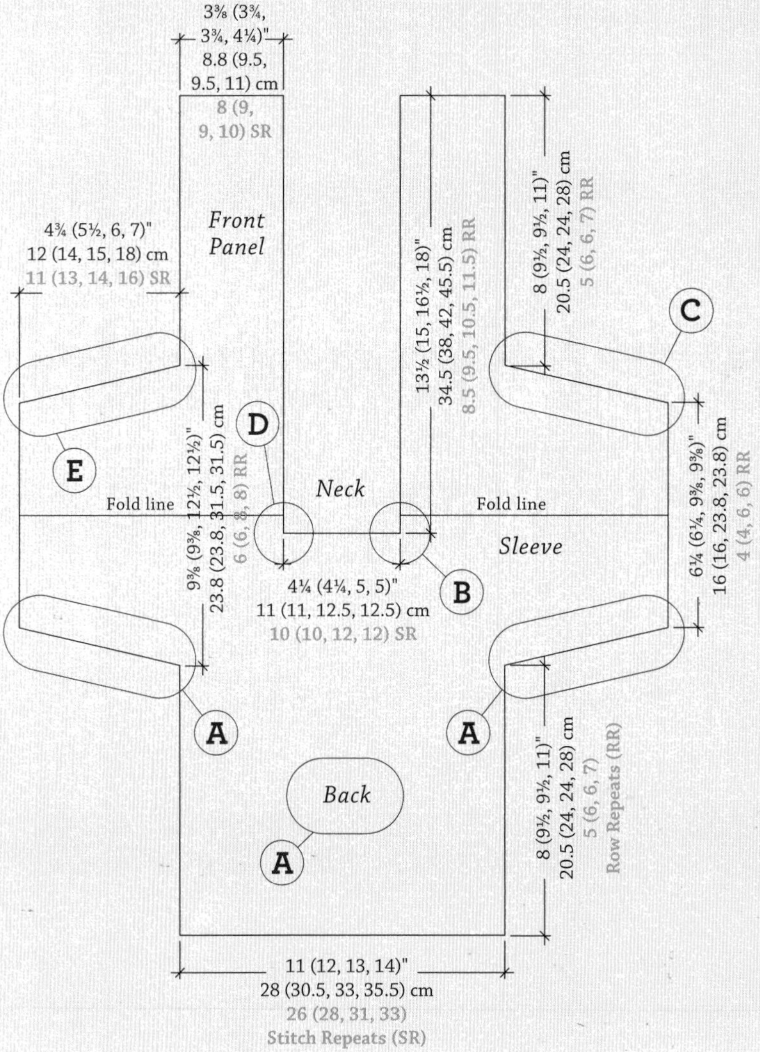

3⅜ (3¾, 3¾, 4¼)"
8.8 (9.5, 9.5, 11) cm
8 (9, 9, 10) SR
Front Panel
4¾ (5½, 6, 7)"
12 (14, 15, 18) cm
11 (13, 14, 16) SR
13½ (15, 16½, 18)"
34.5 (38, 42, 45.5) cm
8.5 (9.5, 10.5, 11.5) RR
8 (9½, 9½, 11)"
20.5 (24, 24, 28) cm
5 (6, 6, 7) RR
C
D
E
Neck
Fold line
Fold line
Sleeve
9⅜ (9⅜, 12½, 12½)"
23.8 (23.8, 31.5, 31.5) cm
6 (6, 8, 8) RR
6¼ (6¼, 9⅜, 9⅜)"
16 (16, 23.8, 23.8) cm
4 (4, 6, 6) RR
4¼ (4¼, 5, 5)"
11 (11, 12.5, 12.5) cm
10 (10, 12, 12) SR
B
A
A
Back
A
8 (9½, 9½, 11)"
20.5 (24, 24, 28) cm
5 (6, 6, 7)
Row Repeats (RR)
11 (12, 13, 14)"
28 (30.5, 33, 35.5) cm
26 (28, 31, 33)
Stitch Repeats (SR)

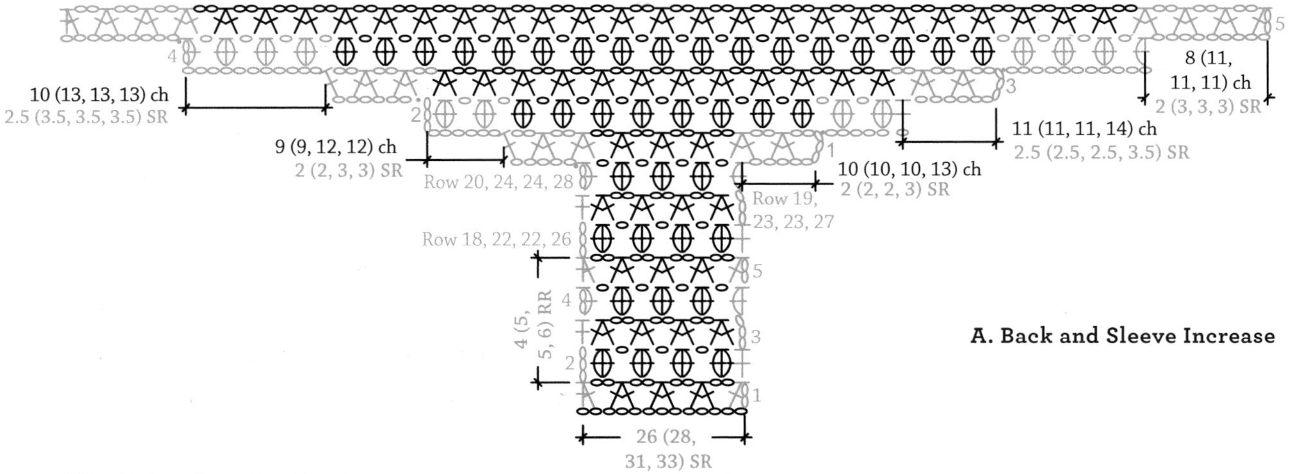

5
4
8 (11, 11, 11) ch
2 (3, 3, 3) SR
10 (13, 13, 13) ch
2.5 (3.5, 3.5, 3.5) SR
3
2
11 (11, 11, 14) ch
2.5 (2.5, 2.5, 3.5) SR
9 (9, 12, 12) ch
2 (2, 3, 3) SR
1
10 (10, 10, 13) ch
2 (2, 2, 3) SR
Row 20, 24, 24, 28
Row 19, 23, 23, 27
Row 18, 22, 22, 26
5
4
4 (5, 5, 6) RR
3
2
1
26 (28, 31, 33) SR

A. Back and Sleeve Increase

Details

CLUSTER STITCH PATTERN (CSP)

See **Cluster Stitch Pattern** diagram below for assistance.

Ch 27.

Row 1(WS): Dc in 4th ch from hook, *ch 2, dc2tog in next ch and 2 ch away (sk one ch), rep from * across to last 2 ch, ch 2, dc2tog in last 2 ch, turn—8 dc2tog.

Row 2: Ch 3, *3dc-cl in next ch-2 sp, ch 1, rep from * across to last ch-2 sp, 3dc-cl in last ch-2 sp, dc in dc, turn—8 3dc-cl.

Row 3: Ch 3, dc2tog in dc and ch-1 sp, *ch 2, dc2tog in same ch-1 sp and next ch-1 sp (sk next 3dc-cl), rep from * across to last ch-1 sp, ch 2, dc2tog in last ch-1 sp and top of tch, dc in top of tch, turn.

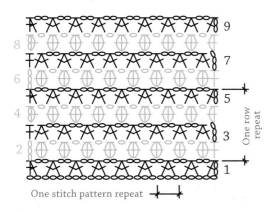

Cluster Stitch Pattern (csp)

NOTES:
Stitch pattern is looser on the first row, then tightens after the second row. Be sure to make a full swatch to determine gauge.

Use larger hook for S and M collar and cuff; use smaller hook for L and XL collar and cuff. Use smaller hook for all sizes of the body.

Row 4: Ch 2, dc in dc, *ch 1, 3dc-cl in next ch-2 sp, rep from * across to last ch-2 sp, ch 1, 2dc-cl in top of tch, turn.

Row 5: Ch 2, dc in ch-1 sp, *ch 2, dc2tog in same ch-1 sp and next ch-1 sp (sk next 3dc-cl), rep from * across to last ch-1 sp, ch 2, dc2tog in last ch-1 sp and dc, turn.

Rep Rows 2–5 to desired length.

Construction

BACK PANEL

See **Stitch Diagram A** on page 66 for assistance.

With MC, ch 81 (87, 96, 102).

Row 1(WS): Dc in 4th ch from hook, *ch 2, dc2tog in next ch and 2 ch away (sk one ch), rep from * across to last 2 ch, ch 2, dc2tog in last 2 ch, turn—26 (28, 31, 33) dc2tog.

Rep Rows 2–5 of csp 4 (5, 5, 6) times. Rep Rows 2–4 of csp once.

Sleeve Increase:

See Stitch Diagram A on page 66 for assistance.

Row 1: Ch 10 (10, 10, 13), lay down working lp, join new ball of MC to end of row with sl st, ch 5 (5, 5, 8), fasten off, pick up working lp, dc2tog in 7th and 9th ch from hook, **(XL only)** ch 2, dc2tog in next ch and 2 ch away (sk one ch), **(All sizes)** ch 2, dc2tog in last ch and next ch-1 sp, ch 2, cont in Row 5 of csp to last ch-1 sp, dc2tog in last ch-1 sp and first ch, ch 2, *dc2tog in next ch and 2 ch away, ch 2, rep from * 0 (0, 0, 1) times, dc in last ch, turn—29 (31, 34, 38) dc2tog.

Row 2: Ch 9 (9, 12, 12), lay down working lp, join new ball of MC to end of row with sl st, ch 6 (6, 9, 9), fasten off, pick up working lp, 3dc-cl in 5th ch from hook, *ch 1, sk 2 ch, 3dc-cl in next ch, rep from * 0 (0, 0, 1) times, cont in Row 2 of csp to last ch-2 sp, 3dc-cl in last ch-2 sp, ch 1, 3dc-cl in ch-6 sp, ch 1, sk first ch, 3dc-cl in next ch, *ch 1, sk 2 ch, 3dc-cl in next ch, rep from * 0 (0 ,0, 1) times, dc in last ch, turn—34 (36, 41, 45) 3dc-cl.

Row 3: Ch 11 (11, 11, 14), lay down working lp, join new ball of MC to end of row with sl st, ch 6 (6, 6, 9), fasten off, pick up working lp, dc2tog in 7th and 9th ch from hook, **(XL only)** ch 2, dc2tog in next ch and 2 ch away (sk one ch), **(All sizes)** ch 2, dc2tog in next ch and dc, ch 2, cont in Row 3 of csp to last ch-1 sp, dc2tog in last ch-1 sp and top of tch, ch 2, dc2tog in top of tch and 2nd ch (sk first ch), ch 2, * dc2tog in next ch and 2 ch away (sk one ch), ch 2, rep from * 0 (0, 0, 1) times, dc in last ch, turn—38 (40, 45, 51) dc2tog.

Row 4: Ch 10 (13, 13, 13), lay down working lp, join new ball of MC to end of row with sl st, ch 8 (11, 11, 11), fasten off, pick up working lp, dc in 3rd ch from hook, *ch 1, sk 2 ch, 3dc-cl in next ch, rep from * 1 (2, 2, 2) times, cont in Row 4 of csp to last ch-2 sp, 3dc-cl in last ch-2 sp, ch 1, 3dc-cl in ch-6 sp, ch 1, sk first ch, 3dc-cl in next ch, *ch 1, sk 2 ch, 3dc-cl in next ch, rep from * 0 (1, 1, 1) times, ch 1, sk 2 ch, 2dc-cl in last ch, turn—43 (47, 52, 58) 3dc-cl.

Row 5: Ch 8 (11, 11, 11), lay down working lp, join new ball of MC to end of row with sl st, ch 6 (9, 9, 9), fasten off, pick up working lp, dc in 4th ch from hook, *ch 2, dc2tog in next ch and 2 ch away (sk one ch), rep from * 0 (1, 1, 1) times, ch 2, dc2tog in last ch and next ch-1 sp, ch 2, cont in Row 5 of csp to last ch-1 sp, dc2tog in last ch-1 sp and first ch, ch 2, * dc2tog in next ch and 2 ch away (sk one ch), ch 2, rep from * 0 (1, 1, 1) times, dc2tog in last 2 ch, turn—48 (54, 59, 65) dc2tog.

Rep Rows 2–5 of csp 1 (1, 2, 2) times. Rep Row 2 of csp.

Neck Opening:

See **Stitch Diagram B** below for assistance.

Row 1: Cont in Row 3 of csp for 19 (22, 23, 26) dc2tog, dc in next ch-1 sp, turn.

Rep Rows 4–5 of csp. Rep Rows 2–5 of csp 1 (1, 2, 2) times.

Rep Rows 2–4 of csp, fasten off.

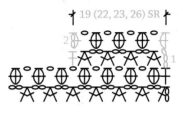

B. Neck

Sleeve Decrease:

See **Stitch Diagram C** below for assistance.

Row 1: Join MC with sl st to 2nd (3rd, 3rd, 3rd) ch-1 sp, ch 2, dc in next ch-1 sp, cont in Row 5 of csp to end, turn—17 (19, 20, 23) dc2tog.

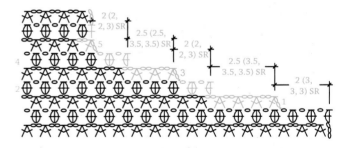

C. Sleeve Decrease

Row 2: Cont in Row 2 of csp across to last 3 (4, 4, 4) ch-2 sps, 2dc-cl in next ch-2 sp, fasten off, turn—15 (16, 17, 20) 3dc-cl.

Row 3: Join MC with sl st to 2nd (2nd, 2nd, 3rd) ch-1 sp, ch 2, dc in next ch-1 sp, cont in Row 3 of csp to end, turn—13 (14, 15, 17) dc2tog.

Row 4: Cont in Row 4 of csp across to last 3 (3, 4, 4) ch-2 sps, 2dc-cl in next ch-2 sp, fasten off, turn—10 (11, 11, 13) 3dc-cl.

Row 5: Join MC with sl st to 2nd (2nd, 2nd, 3rd) ch-1 sp, ch 2, dc in next ch-1 sp, cont in Row 5 of csp to end—8 (9, 9, 10) dc2tog.

FRONT PANEL

Rep Rows 2–5 of csp 4 (5, 5, 6) times. Rep Rows 2–4 of csp once, fasten off, turn.

Opposite Neck Opening:

See **Stitch Diagram D** below for assistance.

Row 1: Join MC to 10th (10th, 12th, 12th) ch-1 sp with sl st, ch 3, cont in Row 3 of csp to end, turn—19 (22, 23, 26) dc2tog.

Rep Rows 4–5 of csp. Rep Rows 2–5 of csp 1 (1, 2, 2) times. Rep Rows 2–4 of csp.

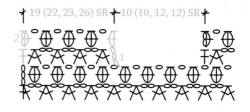

D. Opposite Neck

Opposite Sleeve Decrease:

See **Stitch Diagram E** below for assistance.

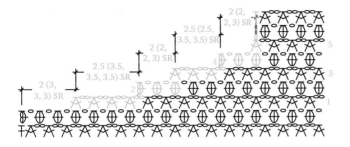

E. Opposite Sleeve Decrease

Row 1: Cont in Row 5 of csp for 17 (19, 20, 23) dc2tog, fasten off, turn.

Row 2: Join MC to 3rd (4th, 4th, 4th) ch-2 sp with sl st, ch 2, dc in same ch-2 sp, cont in Row 2 of csp across to end—14 (15, 16, 19) 3dc-cl.

Row 3: Cont in Row 3 of csp to last 2 (2, 2, 3) ch-1 sps, fasten off, turn—12 (13, 14, 16) dc2tog.

Row 4: Join MC to 3rd (3rd, 4th, 4th) ch-2 sp with sl st, ch 2, dc in same ch-2 sp, cont in Row 4 of csp across to end—10 (11, 11, 13) 3dc-cl.

Row 5: Cont in Row 5 of csp to last 2 (2, 2, 3) ch-1 sps, turn—8 (9, 9, 10) dc2tog.

Opposite Front Panel:

Rep Rows 2–5 of csp 4 (5, 5, 6) times. Rep Rows 2–4 of csp once, fasten off.

Finishing

POSY GRANNY

Follow **Stitch Diagram F** below. Change colors as follows: CC1 on Rnd 1, CC2 on Rnd 2, MC on Rnds 3 and 4. Make 3 Posy Grannies, one for collar and each cuff.

Collar:

Refer to **Joining Diagram G** below and the **Collar Construction Diagram** on page 71 to join 9 (10, 12, 13) more Posy Grannies. The center 4 (3, 3, 4) grannies are joined with their WS facing up.

Cuff (Make 2):

Refer to Joining Diagram G below and the **Cuff Construction Diagram** on page 71 to join 1 (1, 2, 2) more grannies to each cuff granny.

F. Posy Granny

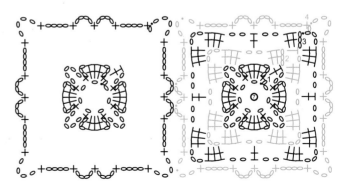

G. Granny Joining

BLOCKING AND SEAMING

Pin body (Back and Front Panels), Collar, and Cuffs to schematic size. Spritz with water and allow to dry. Fold body in half through center of sleeves (at fold line on Plans) matching side and arm seams. With RS facing, whipstitch along arm and side seams. Turn right side out.

EDGING

Join MC with sl st to bottom edge of RS of Back panel, ch 1, sc evenly around the body, sl st to first sc. Fasten off and weave in ends. Rep on arm edge.

ATTACH CUFFS

Unwind one edge of Cuff, join Cuffs as shown on Joining Diagram G. Pin Cuff to arm edge, with RS facing, and whip-stitch in place with leftover yarn. Rep for second Cuff.

ATTACH COLLAR

Pin Collar to neck edge, with RS facing, and whipstitch in place with leftover yarn.

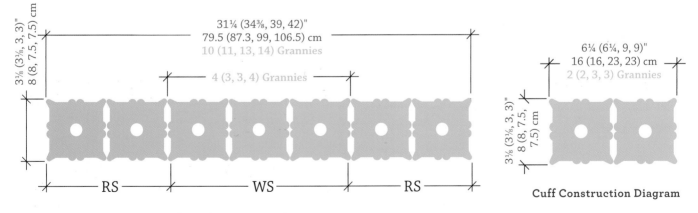

31¼ (34⅜, 39, 42)"
79.5 (87.3, 99, 106.5) cm
10 (11, 13, 14) Grannies

4 (3, 3, 4) Grannies

3⅛ (3⅛, 3, 3)"
8 (8, 7.5, 7.5) cm

— RS — WS — RS —

Collar Construction Diagram

6¼ (6¼, 9, 9)"
16 (16, 23, 23) cm
2 (2, 3, 3) Grannies

3⅛ (3⅛, 3, 3)"
8 (8, 7.5, 7.5) cm

Cuff Construction Diagram

hunter
Pullover

Need a sweater for a winter-themed family photo? Look no further; this cozy sweater will keep your little guy warm and make him look pretty slick. The colorwork crochet gives you a complex look with easy-to-follow instructions. Keep in mind that the colorwork band can easily be modified to any of your favorite images simply by changing where you place your colors. Just use the colorwork diagram as your guide and chart out your favorite image instead.

Equipment

YARN: Sportweight (#2 Fine).

Shown: Tahki/Stacy Charles: Filatura Di Crosa, Zarina (100% lana extrafine merino superwash wool; 181 yd [165 m]/1¾ oz [50 g]): #1651 light yellow (MC), 3 (4, 5, 6) balls; #431 kelly green (CC1), 2 (2, 2, 2) balls; #1734 green (CC2), 1 (1, 1, 1) ball; #1778 bright royal blue (CC3), 1 (1, 1, 1) ball.

HOOK: G/6 (4.00 mm) or hook needed to obtain gauge.

NOTIONS: Tapestry needle for weaving in ends; spray bottle with water and straight pins for blocking; three ½" (1.3 cm) buttons; three size 2 sew-on snaps; 6" (15 cm) of ⅝" (1.5 cm) wide grosgrain ribbon; thread and handsewing needle.

Gauge

22 sts by 30 rows (11 SR by 15 RR)= 4" × 4" (10 × 10 cm) in Spike Stitch Pattern (ssp).

Finished Size

Small (Medium, Large, Extra Large) pullover is sized to fit 6 (12, 18, 24) mths with a relaxed fit. Sample shown is a size Extra Large (24 mths).

Finished Chest: 20 (22½, 25, 27½)" (51 [57, 63.5, 70] cm).

Finished Length: 9⅜ (10⅜, 11½, 13½)" (23.8 [26.3, 29, 34.5] cm).

The Plans

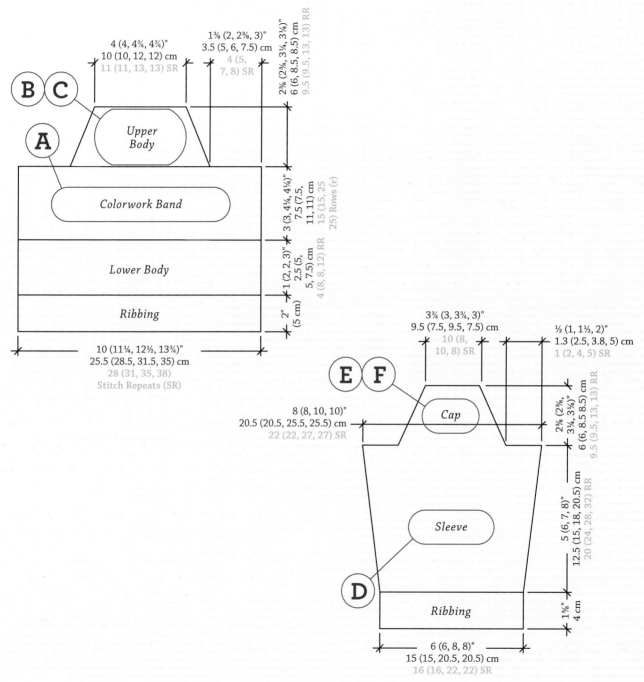

B C

A

Upper Body

4 (4, 4¾, 4¾)"
10 (10, 12, 12) cm
11 (11, 13, 13) SR

1⅜ (2, 2⅜, 3)"
3.5 (5, 6, 7.5) cm
4 (5, 7, 8) SR

2⅜ (2⅜, 3¼, 3¼)"
6 (6, 8.5, 8.5) cm
9.5 (9.5, 13, 13) RR

Colorwork Band

3 (3, 4¼, 4¼)"
7.5 (7.5, 11, 11) cm
15 (15, 25, 25) Rows (r)

Lower Body

1 (2, 2, 3)"
2.5 (5, 5, 7.5) cm
4 (8, 8, 12) RR

Ribbing

2"
(5 cm)

10 (11¼, 12½, 13¾)"
25.5 (28.5, 31.5, 35) cm
28 (31, 35, 38)
Stitch Repeats (SR)

E F

Cap

3¾ (3, 3¾, 3)"
9.5 (7.5, 9.5, 7.5) cm
10 (8, 10, 8) SR

½ (1, 1½, 2)"
1.3 (2.5, 3.8, 5) cm
1 (2, 4, 5) SR

2⅜ (2⅜, 3¼, 3¼)"
6 (6, 8.5 8.5) cm
9.5 (9.5, 13, 13) RR

8 (8, 10, 10)"
20.5 (20.5, 25.5, 25.5) cm
22 (22, 27, 27) SR

Sleeve

5 (6, 7, 8)"
12.5 (15, 18, 20.5) cm
20 (24, 28, 32) RR

D

Ribbing

1⅝"
4 cm

6 (6, 8, 8)"
15 (15, 20.5, 20.5) cm
16 (16, 22, 22) SR

Details

SPIKE STITCH PATTERN (SSP)

Insert hook into st indicated 1 row below (over ch-1 sp), yo, pull up a lp, yo, pull through all loops on hook.

See **Spike Stitch Pattern** diagram below for assistance.

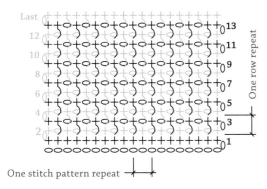

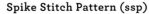

Spike Stitch Pattern (ssp)

Spike Stitch Pattern in Rows:

Ch 24.

Row 1(RS): Sc in 2nd ch from the hook and in ea ch across, turn—23 sc, 11 SR.

Row 2: Ch 1, sc in first sc, *ch 1, sk 1 sc, sc in next sc, rep from * across to end, turn.

Row 3: Ch 1, sc in first sc, *sc spike in next sc 1 row below (over ch-1 sp), ch 1, sk next sc, rep from * across to last 2 sts, sc spike in next sc 1 row below, sc in last sc, turn.

Row 4: Ch 1, sc in first sc, *ch 1, sk next sc, sc spike in next sc one row below, rep from * around to last st, ch 1, sk next sc, sc in last sc, turn.

Rep Rows 3–4 for pattern.

Spike Stitch Pattern in Rnds:

Ch an odd number of sts.

Rnd 1(RS): Sc in 2nd ch from the hook and in ea ch across, sl st to first sc, turn.

Rnd 2: Ch 1, sc in first sc, ch 1, sk 1 sc, *sc in next sc, ch 1, sk 1 sc, rep from * around, sl st to first sc, turn.

Rnd 3: Ch 1, sk first sc, *sc spike in next sc 1 row below (over ch-1 sp), ch 1, sk next sc, rep from * around to last st, sc spike in next sc 1 row below, sl st in first sc, turn.

Rep Rnd 3 for pattern.

Construction

BODY

Snowflake Band:

Ch 113 (127, 141, 155) with CC1.

Rnd 1(RS): Sc in 2nd ch from hook and ea ch across, sl st to first sc, turn—112 (126, 140, 154) sc (56 [63, 70, 77] SR).

(L/XL only): Rep Rnds 2–3 of ssp once, then Rnd 3 twice more, changing colors as shown on ea rnd in **Stitch Diagram A** (on page 76) sl st to first sc at end of ea rnd, turn.

Rnd 6: Change to CC1, ch 1, sc in first sc, *sc spike in next sc 1 row below, sc in next sc, rep from * around, sl st to first sc, turn.

(ALL): Note: Sizes M and XL will have an odd number of snowflake motifs; therefore, there will be 2 MC motifs side-by-side at beginning and end of rnds.

Follow Stitch Diagram A, changing colors as shown for 14 rnds, sl st to first st of ea rnd, turn.

(L/XL only): Rep Rnds 2–3 of ssp once, then Rnd 3 twice more, changing colors as shown on ea row in Stitch Diagram A, sl st to first sc at end of ea rnd, turn.

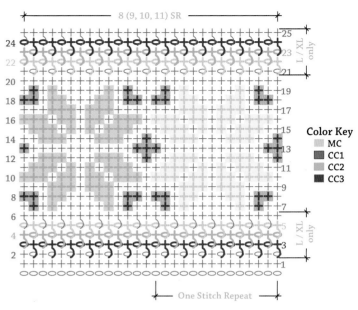

A. Band Colorwork

Rnd 25: Change to CC1, ch 1, sc in first sc, sc spike in next sc
1 row below, *sc in next sc, sc spike in next sc 1 row below,
rep from * around, sl st to first sc, turn.

Lower Body:

Change to MC.

Rnd 1: Rep Rnd 2 of ssp around, sl st to first sc, turn—56
(63, 70, 77) SR.

Rep Rnd 3 of ssp 6 (14, 14, 22) times, sl st to first sc on ea
rnd, turn.

Last Rnd: Ch 1, sc in first sc, *sc spike in next sc 1 row below,
sc in next sc, rep from * around, sl st to first sc, turn.

Ribbing:

Ch 12 with MC.

Row 1: Sc in 2nd ch from hook and in ea ch across, sl st in
next 2 sts of body (first sl st joins ribbing to body, second
counts as a tch), turn—11 sc.

Row 2: Sk sl sts, sc-blp in ea sc across, turn.

Row 3: Ch 1, sc-blp in ea sc across, sl st in next 2 sts of body, turn.

Rep Rows 2–3 evenly around body, fasten off, weave in ends. With tapestry needle, whipstitch ribbing seams together.

Upper Front:

With RS facing, working across top edge of Body, join yarn 3 (10, 9, 16) sts from beginning with a sl st to the next ch of the foundation ch.

Row 1: Ch 1, sc in next 41 (41, 43, 43) sc, leave rem sts un-worked, turn—20 (20, 21, 21) SR.

Cont with **Stitch Diagram B (B, C, C)** below for 19 (19, 26, 26) rows, fasten off—11 (11, 13, 13) SR.

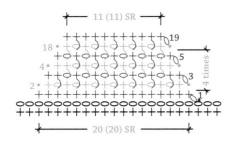

B. S/M Upper Body Shaping

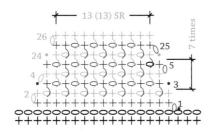

C. L/XL Upper Body Shaping

Upper Back:

Join yarn 14 (21, 26, 33) sts from end of Row 1 of the Upper Front with a sl st to the next ch of the foundation ch.

Row 1: Ch 1, sc in next 41 (41, 43, 43) sc, leave rem sts unworked, turn—20 (20, 21, 21) SR.

Cont with Stitch Diagram B (B, C, C) for 19 (19, 26, 26) rows, fasten off—11 (11, 13, 13) SR.

SLEEVE (MAKE 2)

Ch 34 (34, 46, 46) with MC.

Row 1(RS): Sc in 2nd ch from hook and in ea ch across, turn—33 (33, 45, 45) sc, 16 (16, 22, 22) SR.

Row 2: Ch 1, sc in first sc, *ch 1, sk 1 sc, sc in next sc, rep from * across to end, turn.

(M/XL only) Rep Rows 3–4 of ssp twice.

Arm Increase:

See **Stitch Diagram D** at right for assistance.

Row 1: Ch 1, 2 sc in first sc, cont in ssp across to last sc, 2 sc in last sc, turn—17 (17, 23, 23) SR.

Rows 2–7 (2–7, 2–13, 2–13): Rep Rows 3–4 of ssp 3 (3, 6, 6) times.

Rep Rows 1–7 (1–7, 1–13, 1–13) 4 (4, 3, 3) times.

Last Row: Ch 1, 2 sc in first sc, cont in ssp across to last sc, 2 sc in last sc, turn—22 (22, 27, 27) SR.

Arm Cap:

See **Stitch Diagram E (E, F, F)** at right for assistance.

(M/XL only): Rep Rows 3–4 of ssp twice.

Row 1 (S/M only): Rep Row 3 of ssp once.

Row 2 (S/M only): Ch 1, sc in next sc, *sc in next sc, sc spike over next sc 1 row below *, rep from * to * 0 (1) times, cont in ssp across to last 3 (5) sts, sc spike over next sc 1 row below, rep from * to * 0 (1) times, sc in last 2 sc, turn.

Row 3 (S/M only): Sl st in next 3 (5) sc, cont in ssp across to last 3 (5) sc, leave rem sts unworked, turn.

Row 1 (L/XL only): Ch 1, sc in next sc, *sc spike over next sc 1 row below, sc in next sc *, rep from * to * 3 (4) more times, cont in ssp across to last 10 (12) sts, rep from * to * 5 (6) times, turn.

Row 2 (L/XL only): Sl st in next 9 (11) sc, cont in ssp across to last 9 (11) sc, leave rem sts unworked, turn.

(All): Cont in Stitch Diagram E (E, F, F) to end, fasten off, weave in ends.

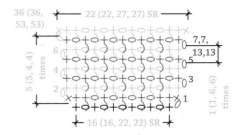

D. Sleeve Shaping

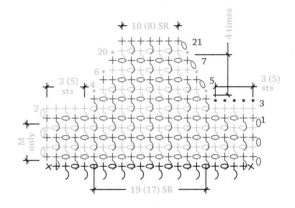

E. S/M Cap Shaping

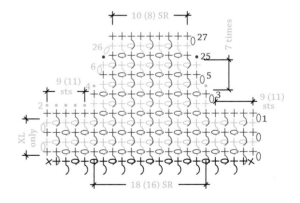

F. L/XL Cap Shaping

Finishing

Pin body and sleeves to schematic size (see the Plans on page 74). Spritz with water and allow to dry.

RAGLAN SEAM

Join MC to WS edge of back panel left seam or right front panel seam with sl st.

Row 1: Ch 1, sc evenly down raglan edge, sl st in next 2 sts on armhole edge, fasten off MC, turn.

Row 2: Join CC1, sk 1 sl st, sc in next sl st, sc in ea sc across, turn.

Row 3: Ch 1, sc in ea sc across to last sc, 2 sc in last sc, sl st in next 2 sts on armhole edge, turn.

Rep Rows 2–3 once, fasten off.

Join MC to WS edge of back panel right seam or left front panel seam with sl st.

Row 1: Ch 1, sc evenly up raglan edge, fasten off, turn.

Row 2: Join CC1, ch 1, sc in ea sc across, 2 sc in last sc, sl st in next 2 sts on armhole edge, turn.

Row 3: Sk 1 sl st, sc in next sl st, sc in ea sc across, turn.

Rep Rows 2–3 once, fasten off.

Join MC to WS edge of left sleeve seam on left sleeve with sl st.

Row 1: Ch 1, sc evenly up raglan edge, fasten off MC, turn.

Row 2: Join CC1, ch 1, sc in ea sc across, turn.

Rep Row 2 three times, fasten off.

Join MC to edge of WS of rem sleeve raglan edges. Sc evenly up raglan edge, fasten off.

SEAMING

Pin RS of Sleeves and Body together. Whipstitch arm and side seams together with leftover yarn. Turn right side out.

CUFFS

Join MC to edge of sleeve, ch 10.

Row 1: Sc in 2nd ch from hook and ea ch across, sl st in next 2 sts on sleeve (first sl st joins ribbing to sleeve, second counts as a tch), turn—9 sc.

Row 2: Sk sl sts, sc-blp in each sc across, turn.

Row 3: Ch 1, sc-blp in ea sc across, sl st in next 2 sts on sleeve, turn.

Rep Rows 2–3 evenly around sleeve, fasten off, weave in ends.

With tapestry needle, whipstitch ribbing seams together. Rep Cuff on other sleeve.

COLLAR

With RS facing, join CC1 to RS edge of neck with sl st.

Row 1: Ch 1, sc evenly across neck edge, turn.

Row 2: Ch 1, sc in ea sc across, turn.

Rep Row 2 three times.

Sew buttons to raglan seam on right side edge of Front, placing first button ½" (1.3 cm) below top edge, bottom button 1½" (3.8 cm) above bottom edge of raglan seam, and third button evenly spaced between. Cut the grosgrain ribbon in half. Using the thread and handsewing needle, sew one half of each snap to each piece of ribbon securely, centering the snaps and leaving the same gap between the snaps as you left between the buttons. Sew the ribbons to the inside of the raglan, corresponding to the button placement. Be sure to fold under the short edges of the ribbon as you stitch it down to hide the raw edges.

Accessories

Aa any style expert will tell you, it's all about choosing the right accessories to pull off a new outfit. Well, it's not different with new crochet techniques: all you need are the right accessories. Each of the fantastic baby accessories in this chapter will bring you one step closer to being a symbol crochet master. Plus, all are really tiny projects that you can complete in a day. Just think of what you could learn in a week of crocheting! When you're done, some lucky baby will be able to crawl or toddle away as the best-dressed kiddo on the block!

snuggly Socks

One of the best gifts for babies, both to give and to receive, is socks. Parents constantly find that they are losing socks, and of course, we all know that the dryer eats them. So, you can just never have too many pairs of socks to keep baby's toes nice and warm. Besides, is there anything cuter than tiny socks? This project includes instructions for two variations, both of which are made with an incredibly snuggly, stretchy wool yarn. Make a set or two for the next baby shower you attend; you know they will be a big hit!

Equipment

YARN: Fingering weight (#1 Super Fine).

Shown: Classic Elite Yarns, Summer Sox (40% cotton, 40% superwash merino, 20% nylon; 175 yd [160 m]/ 1.7 oz [50 g]): #5557 pelican (MC), 1 ball; #5581 seagrass (CC), 1 ball.

HOOK: E/5 (3.5 mm) or hook needed to obtain gauge.

NOTIONS: Tapestry needle for weaving in ends; stitch markers.

Gauge

22 esc by 20 rows = 4" × 4" (10 × 10 cm).

Finished Size

Small (Medium, Large) socks are sized to fit 0–6 (6–12, 12–24) mths. Socks shown are size Medium (6–12 mths).

The Plans

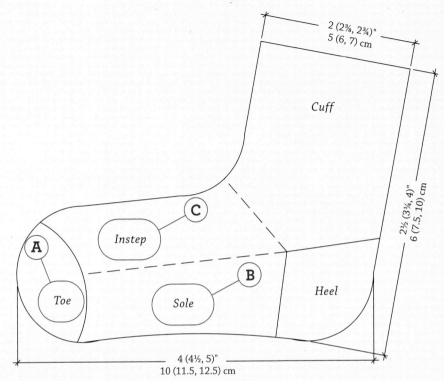

2 (2⅜, 2¾)"
5 (6, 7) cm

Cuff

2½ (3¼, 4)"
6 (7.5, 10) cm

C

Instep

A

Toe

B

Sole

Heel

4 (4½, 5)"
10 (11.5, 12.5) cm

NOTE: There is an optional stitch pattern for the instep and cuff of the sock. You can follow instructions for the basic sock all the way through or use the optional stitch pattern for some contrast in the instep and cuff. Please read the directions carefully for the optional stitch pattern on page 86 before starting the instep.

Construction (Make 2)

TOE

See **Stitch Diagram A** below for assistance.

Ch 6, 7, 8 with CC.

Rnd 1(RS): Esc in third ch from hook (sk ch count as esc), esc in ea ch across to last ch, 3 esc in last ch, pm in first and third esc, (rotate work 180 degrees and now work in opp side of foundation ch), esc in ea ch across, sl st to tch, turn—10 (12, 14) esc.

Rnd 2: Ch 2 (count as esc), 2 esc in next esc, pm in second esc, esc in ea esc to m, 2 esc in next esc, pm in first esc, esc in next esc, 2 esc in next esc, pm in second esc, esc in ea esc to last, 2 esc in last esc, pm in first esc, sl st to tch, turn—14 (16, 18) esc.

Rnd 3: Ch 2 (count as esc), esc in next esc, 2 esc in next esc, *esc in ea esc to m, 2 esc in next esc, rep from * twice, esc in next esc, sl st to tch, turn—18 (20, 22) esc.

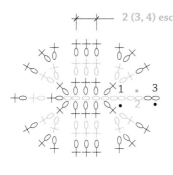

A. Toe

ARCH INCREASE

See **Stitch Diagram B** below for assistance.

Fasten off CC and join MC.

Rnd 1(WS): Ch 2 (count as esc), esc in next esc and ea esc around, sl st to tch, turn.

Rnd 2: Ch 2 (count as esc), esc in next 3 (4, 5) esc, 3 esc in next esc, pm in first and third esc and move marker up as work progresses, esc in ea esc to end, sl st to tch, turn—20 (22, 24) esc.

Rnds 3–4: Rep Rnd 1.

Rnd 5: Ch 2 (count as esc), esc in ea esc across to m, 2 esc in next esc, pm in first esc and move marker up as work progresses, esc in ea esc to m, 2 esc in next esc, pm in second esc and move marker up as work progresses, esc in ea esc to end, sl st to tch; turn—22 (24, 26) esc.

Rep Rnds 3–5 one (two, three) times—24 (28, 32) esc.

Rep Rnd 1 two (one, zero) times.

Last Rnd: Ch 2 (count as esc), esc in next 10 (12, 14) esc, ch 11 (13, 15) (forms heel opening), sk rem esc across, sl st to tch, turn.

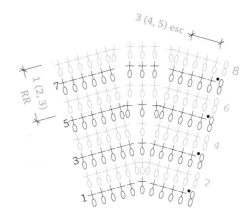

B. Sole

Row 5 (6, 7): Ch 5 (6, 7), sc in 2nd ch from hook and ea ch across, sl st in next 2 sts on top of sock (once to join ribbing to cuff, and once for a tch), turn—4 (5, 6) sc.

Row 6 (7, 8): Sk 2 sl st, sc-blp in ea sc across, turn.

Row 7 (8, 9): Ch 1, sc-blp in ea sc across, sl st in next 2 sts on top of sock, turn.

Rep prev 2 rows around top of sock. Fasten off, leaving long tail. Whipstitch tail through ends of ribbing to close.

OPTIONAL ARCH

Do not fasten off CC. Divide sts in half into Sole sts and Instep sts.

Note: Place marker if it helps to keep sts organized. Follow directions for Arch Increase for sole only; inc as described.

Instep Stitches of Arch:

See **Stitch Diagram C** below for assistance.

Instep Even Rnds(RS): Cont in Arch Increase as est to last 8 (9, 10) sts, ch 1, sk 3 sts, dc in next st, ch 1, dc in second skipped st, ch 1, sk next st, esc in ea esc to end, sl st to tch, turn.

Instep Odd Rnds (WS): Ch 2 (counts as esc), esc in ea esc to ch-1 sp, esc in ch-1 sp, sk next dc, 3 sc in next ch-1 sp, sk next dc, esc in last ch-1 sp, cont in Arch Increase to end, turn.

CUFF

See Optional Cuff on page 87 if you prefer.

Rnd 1(RS): Ch 2 (count as esc), esc in ea ch across, esc in ea esc across, sl st to tch, turn—22 (26, 30) esc.

Rnd 2: Ch 2 (count as esc), esc in next esc and ea esc around, sl st to tch, turn.

Rep Rnd 2 two (three, four) times. Fasten off MC and join CC.

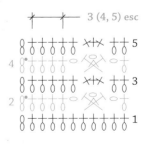

C. Optional Instep

Last Rnd: Ch 2 (count as esc), esc in ea esc to ch-1 sp, esc in ch-1 sp, sk next dc, 3 sc in next ch-1 sp, sk next dc, esc in last ch-1 sp, esc in next 2 (3, 4) esc, ch 11 (13, 15) (forms heel opening), sk rem esc across, sl st to tch, turn.

OPTIONAL CUFF

Rnd 1(RS): Ch 2 (count as esc), esc in ea ch across, esc in ea esc across to last 8 (9, 10) sts, ch 1, sk 3 sts, dc in next st, ch 1, dc in second sk st, ch 1, esc in ea esc to end, sl st to tch, turn—22 (26, 30) sts.

Rnd 2: Ch 2 (counts as esc), *esc in ea esc to ch-1 sp, esc in ch-1 sp, sk next dc, 3 sc in next ch-1 sp, sk next dc, esc in next ch-1 sp, rep from * once, esc in ea esc to end, sl st to tch, turn.

Rnd 3: Ch 2 (counts as esc), esc in next 3 (4, 5) esc, *ch 1, sk 3 sts, dc in next st, ch 1, dc in second skipped st, ch 1*, esc in ea esc to last 8 (9, 10) sts, rep from * to * once, esc in ea esc to end, sl st to tch, turn.

Rep Rnd 2–3 three (three, four) times. Rep Rnd 2 once.

Last Rnd: Ch 1, *sc in next st, ch 2, sc in next sc, rep from * around, sl st to first sc, fasten off.

HEEL

With RS facing, at start of the last rnd of the Arch increase, join CC with sl st around the post of the tch.

Rnd 1(RS): Ch 1, sc around the post of tch, sc in next esc and ea esc across bottom of heal opening to junction, sc around the post of next esc, pm in sc, sc in next ch and ea ch across top of heal opening, sl st to first sc, sl st to next sc, turn—26 (30, 34) sc.

Rnd 2: Ch 1, sc3tog over (2 sl st, sc), sc in ea sc to 1 sc before m, sc3tog over next 3 sc, pm in sc3tog, sc in next sc and ea sc across to end, sl st to first sc, sl st to next sc, turn—22 (26, 30) sc.

Rep Rnd 2 three (four, five) times.

Turn sock inside out, sl st through both sides of fabric across heel, fasten off, weave in ends.

pea pod
Slider Slippers

Finding cute and unique shoes or clothes for little boys can sometimes be frustrating. I know this firsthand from trying to shop for my five nephews, so my solution is crochet. Whenever I can't find something to buy, I create something instead. These comfortable shoes were my recent solution for trying to find some retro-cool soft slippers. This project gives you the option to create the slippers with either a softer or a sturdier sole to fit the recipient's needs. These will be such a hit that all the grown-ups are going to be jealous!

Equipment

YARN: DK weight (#3 Light).

Shown: Lion Brand, LB Collection Cotton Bamboo (52% cotton, 48% rayon from bamboo; 245 yd [224 m]/ 3.5 oz [100 g]): #487-174 snapdragon (MC), 1 ball; CC #487-126 chocolate dahlia (CC), 1 ball.

HOOK: G/6 (4.00 mm) or hook needed to obtain gauge.

NOTIONS: Tapestry needle for weaving in ends; lightweight cardboard (for optional sturdier sole).

Gauge

25 sts by 14 rows = 4" × 4" (10 × 10 cm) in hdc.

Finished Size

Small (Medium, Large) shoes are sized to fit 0–6 mths at 4" (10 cm) long × 2" (5 cm) wide (6–12 months at 4 ½" [11.5 cm] long × 2" [5 cm] wide, 12–24 mths at 5" [12.5 cm] long × 2 ¼" [5.5 cm] wide). Shoes shown are size Medium (6–12 mths).

NOTES:

Instructions are given for size Small (Medium, Large) with the instructions given in parenthesis applied to the Medium and Larges sizes respectively.

The optional sturdier sole is recommended for a walking baby, while the softer sole will work just fine for a crawling baby.

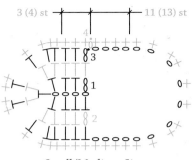

Small/Medium Size

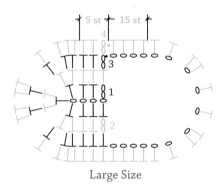

Large Size

A. Instep

Construction (Make 2)

INSTEP

See **Stitch Diagram A** at right for assistance.

With MC, ch 6 (7, 8).

Rnd 1(RS): Hdc in 4th ch from hook (skipped ch count as hdc), hdc in ea ch across to last ch, 3 hdc in last ch, rotate work 180 degrees, hdc in ea ch across to end, turn—9 (11, 13) hdc.

Rnd 2: Ch 2 (count as hdc), hdc in next 2 (3, 4) hdc, 2 hdc in next 3 hdc, hdc in ea hdc across, turn—12 (14, 16) hdc.

Rnd 3: Ch 2 (count as hdc), hdc in next 2 (3, 4) hdc, 2 hdc in next hdc, hdc in next 4 hdc, 2 hdc in next hdc, hdc in ea hdc across, ch 30 (34, 38), sl st to top of tch, do not turn—14 (16, 18) hdc.

Rnd 4: Ch 1 (1, 2), **(S, M only)** sc in top of tch, **(All)** work sc (sc, hdc) in next 2 (3, 4) hdc, 2 sc (sc, hdc) in next hdc, sc (sc, hdc) in next 2 hdc, 2 sc (2 sc, 2 hdc) in next 2 hdc, sc (sc, hdc) in next 2 hdc, 2 sc (2 sc, 2 hdc) in next hdc, sc (sc, hdc) in ea hdc across, sc (sc, hdc) in next 13 (15, 17) ch, 2 sc, (2 sc, 2 hdc) in next ch, sc (sc, hdc) in next 2 ch, 2 sc (2 sc, 2 hdc) in next ch, sc (sc, hdc) in ea ch across to end, sl st to first sc, (sc, top of tch), do not turn—50 sc (56 sc, 62 hdc).

SIDES

Rnd 1(RS): Ch 2 (count as hdc), hdc-blp in ea st around, sl st to top of tch, do not turn.

Rnd 2: Ch 2 (count as hdc), hdc in ea st around, sl st to top of tch, do not turn.

Rnd 3: Ch 1 (2, 2), **(S only)** sc in top of tch, **(All sizes)** sc, (hdc, hdc) in ea st around, sl st to first sc (top of tch, top of tch), do not turn, fasten off MC.

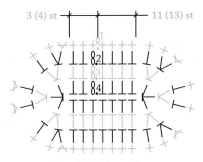

3 (4) st — 11 (13) st

Small/Medium Size

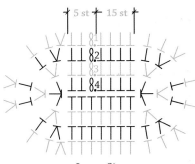

5 st — 15 st

Large Size

B. Exterior Sole

EXTERIOR SOLE

See **Stitch Diagram B** at right for assistance.

Join CC.

Rnd 1(RS): Ch 1 (1, 2), **(S, M only)** sc in top of tch, **(All)** sc-blp (sc-blp, hdc-blp) in next 2 (3, 4) sts, sc2tog-blp (sc2tog-blp, hdc2tog-blp) over next 2 sts, sc-blp (sc-blp, hdc-blp) in next 2 sts, [sc2tog-blp (sc2tog-blp, hdc2tog-blp) over next 2 sts] twice, sc-blp (sc-blp, hdc-blp) in next 2 sts, sc2tog-blp (sc2tog-blp, hdc2tog-blp) over next 2 sts, sc-blp (sc-blp, hdc-blp) in next 16 (19, 22) sts, sc2tog-blp (sc2tog-blp, hdc2tog-blp) over next 2 sts, sc-blp (sc-blp, hdc-blp) in next 2 sts, sc2tog-blp (sc2tog-blp, hdc2tog-blp) over next 2 sts, sc-blp (sc-blp, hdc-blp) in ea st across to end, sl st to first sc (first sc, top of tch), do not turn—44 sc (50 sc, 56 hdc).

Rnd 2: Ch 2 (count as hdc), hdc in next 2 (3, 4) sts, hdc2tog over next 2 sts, hdc in next 4 sts, hdc2tog over next 2 sts, hdc in next 15 (18, 21) st, hdc2tog over next 2 sts, hdc in next 2 sts, hdc2tog over next 2 sts, hdc in ea st across to end, sl st to top of tch, do not turn—40 (46, 52) hdc.

Rnd 3: Ch 2 (count as hdc), hdc in next 2 (3, 4) sts, [hdc2tog over next 2 sts] 3 times, hdc in next 14 (17, 20) sts, [hdc2tog over next 2 sts] 3 times, hdc in ea st across to end, sl st to top of tch, do not turn—34 (40, 46) hdc.

Rnd 4: Ch 2 (count as hdc), hdc in next 2 (3, 4) st, hdc3tog over next 3 sts, hdc in next 14 (17, 20) st, hdc3tog over next 3 sts, hdc in ea st across to end, sl st to top of tch, fasten off, leaving long tail—30 (36, 42) hdc.

Using tapestry needle, whipstitch opening closed with yarn tail; weave in ends.

TONGUE

Join MC to RS of edge of Instep with sl st.

Row 1: Sc across edge of rnds to end, turn.

Row 2: Sl st in first sc, sc in ea sc to last sc, sl st to last sc, turn.

Row 3: Sk sl st, sl st in next sc, sc in ea sc to last sc, sl st to last sc, turn.

Rows 4–5: Rep Row 3, fasten off, weave in ends.

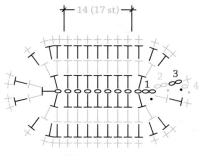

Small/Medium Size

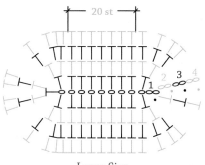

Large Size

C. Interior Sole

OPTIONAL INTERIOR SOLE

With CC, ch 18 (21, 24).

Follow **Stitch Diagram C** below for 4 rnds; fasten off, leaving long tail.

Finishing

OPTIONAL SOLE INSERT

Measure and draw two 4" (10 cm) long × 2" (5 cm) wide (4½" [11.5 cm] long × 2" [5 cm] wide, 5" [12.5 cm] long × 2¼" [5.5 cm] wide) ovals on lightweight cardboard and cut out. Place cardboard in slippers, cover with interior sole (RS facing up). Turn slipper inside out. Whipstitch interior sole into slippers. Turn slipper right side out.

SEAMING AND EDGING

(All) Join CC to Rnd 3 of Side of slipper in front loop not used, sl st in ea st around, fasten off, weave in ends. Join CC to Rnd 3 of Instep at back of slipper, sl st in ea ch across to Tongue, sc across the Tongue, sl st in ea ch around to beg, sl st to first sl st, fasten off, weave in ends.

popsicle
Boots

There is just something about little girls and their boots. Each of my nieces has a favorite pair. For one it's her pink cowboy boots, another has her yellow rain galoshes, and for another it's her comfy Ugg boots. For the ones featured here, I went with bright colors mixed with super-soft yarn, in the hope that they can become your little one's favorite boots. The faux leather sole gives a little grip and structure to the boot, which is helpful for new walkers.

Equipment

YARN: Fingering weight (#1 Superfine).

Shown: Spud and Chloë, Fine (80% superwash wool, 20% silk; 248 yd [227 m]/2.3 oz [65 g]): #7808 sassafras (MC), 1(1, 1) hank; #7801 glow worm (CC1) 1 (1, 1) hank; #7804 cricket (CC2), 1 (1, 1) hank; #7805 anemone (CC3), 1 (1, 1) hank; #7802 clementine (CC4), 1 (1, 1) hank.

HOOK: E/4 (3.50 mm) or hook needed to obtain gauge and 1.00 mm steel hook.

NOTIONS: Tapestry needle for weaving in ends; tracing paper; fabric marker; 6" (15 cm) square of faux leather fabric; sharp leather handsewing needle; six ⅜" (1 cm) buttons; 6 size 1 snaps; 6" (15 cm) of ⅜" (1 cm) wide grosgrain ribbon; matching thread and hand-sewing needle.

Gauge

22 sc by 28 rows = 4" × 4" (10 × 10 cm).

Finished Size

Small (Medium, Large) boots are sized to fit 0–6 (6–12, 12–24) mths. Finished sole is 4 (4½, 5)" (10 [11.5, 12.5] cm) long × 2 (2⅛, 2¼)" (5 [5.4, 5.5] cm) wide. Boots shown are size Small (0–6 mths).

Details

SC Spike (single crochet spike): Insert hook into st indicated 2 rows below, yo, pull up a lp, yarn over, pull through all loops on hook.

Construction

SOLE

Copy the appropriate size sole template onto tracing paper and cut out, then transfer to the wrong side of faux leather with fabric marker. Cut out 2 soles. Mark 54 (60, 66) dots, spaced about $^3/_{16}$" (5 mm) apart, around perimeter of sole and about $^1/_{16}$" (2 mm) from edge. Poke hole at each dot with leather needle. Join MC to hole at center back of sole with 1.00 mm steel hook and sl st. Ch 1, sc in each hole around sole with 1.00 mm steel hook (be careful not to pull too tightly—if it is too difficult to keep stitches loose enough, only use steel hook to get MC through hole, then use E/4 [3.5 mm] hook to finish stitch), sl st to first sc, do not turn—54 (60, 66) sc.

SIDES

Cont with E/4 (3.5 mm) hook.

Rnd 1 (RS): Ch 1, sc-blp in ea sc around, sl st to first sc, do not turn.

Rnd 2: Ch 1, sc in ea sc around, sl st to first sc, do not turn.

Rep Rnd 2 two (three, four) times.

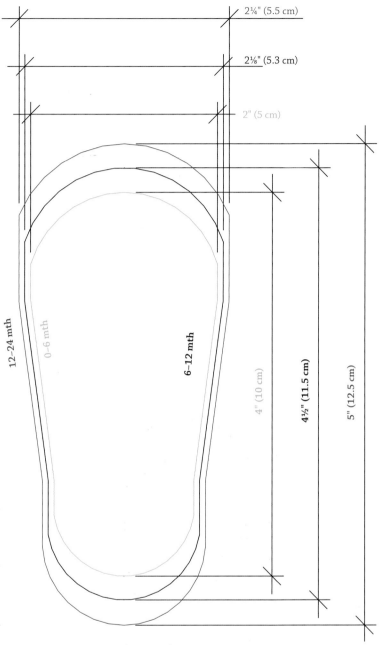

2¼" (5.5 cm)

2⅛" (5.3 cm)

2" (5 cm)

12–24 mth

0–6 mth

6–12 mth

4" (10 cm)

4½" (11.5 cm)

5" (12.5 cm)

Sole Template

INSTEP

See **Stitch Diagram A** below for assistance.

Rnd 1 (RS): Ch 1, sc in next 21 (24, 27) sc, sc2tog over next 4 sc, sc in next 4 sc, sc2tog over next 4 sc, sc in ea sc to end, sl st to first sc, do not turn—50 (56, 62) sc.

Rnd 2: Ch 1, sc in next 21 (24, 27) sc, sc2tog over next 2 sc, sc in next 4 sc, sc2tog over next 2 sc, sc in ea sc to end, sl st to first sc, fasten off—48 (54, 60) sc.

Rnd 3: Sk 13 (15, 17) sc, join MC to next sc with sl st, ch 1, sc in next 3 (4, 5) sc, *sc2tog over next 2 sc, sc in next 2 sc, rep from * twice more, sc2tog over next 2 sc, sc in next 3 (4, 5) sc, leave rem sts unworked, turn—16 (18, 20) sc.

Rnd 4: Ch 1, sc in next 4 (5, 6) sc, *sc2tog over next 2 sc, sc in next sc, rep from * once, sc2tog over next 2 sc, sc in ea sc to end, turn—13 (15, 17) sc.

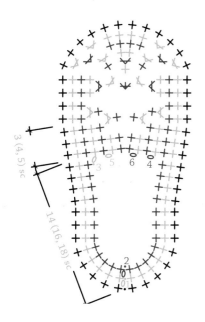

A. Instep Decreases

Rnd 5: Ch 1, sc in next 2 (3, 4) sc, [sc2tog over next 2 sc] twice, sc in next sc, [sc2tog over next 2 sc] twice, sc in ea sc to end, turn—9 (11, 13) sc.

Rnd 6: Ch 1, sc in next 3 (4, 5) sc, sc3tog over next 3 sc, sc in ea sc to end, fasten off, leave long tail—7 (9, 11) sc.
With tapestry needle and holding last rnd together, whipstitch tail through sts to join rnd, weave in ends.

LEFT BOOT BODY

Row 1: With WS facing, join yarn with sl st-flp 3 sc from front of boot at left side, ch 1, sc-flp in same sc, sc-flp in next 3 (3, 5) sc to form back flap, work 36 (42, 46) sc evenly spaced around boot to beg, working in rem free lps of beg sts, sc-blp in next 4 (4, 6) sc to form front flap, turn—40 (46, 52) sc.

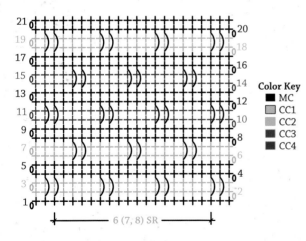

B. Boot Body Colorwork

RIGHT BOOT BODY

Row 1: With WS facing, join yarn with sl st-blp 6 (6, 8) sc from front of boot at right side, ch 1, sc-blp in same sc, sc-blp in next 3 (3, 5) sc to form front flap, work 36 (42, 46) sc evenly space around boot to beg, working in rem free lps of beg sts, sc-flp in next 4 (4, 6) sc to form back flap, turn—40 (46, 52) sc.

Follow **Stitch Diagram B** at left for next 20 rows, alternating location of sc spike as shown. Change color in following order: 2 rows each of CC1, MC, CC2, MC, CC3, MC, CC4, MC, CC1, MC. Fasten off.

Join MC, with RS facing, to edge of boot at row ends, sc evenly up edge of boot to top, 3 sc at top corner, sc in ea sc across to last sc, 3 sc in last sc, sc evenly down edge, fasten off, weave in ends.

Finishing

Cut grosgrain ribbon in half and fold short ends under so that ribbon length matches the length of side opening (this will also ensure that raw edges don't show). With handsewing needle and thread, whipstitch one ribbon to inside of front flap (with folded-under raw edges sandwiched between the layers). Whipstitch other ribbon to top of back flap. Sew buttons evenly down RS of front flap. Sew snaps to opposite side of fabric behind buttons and to back flap in corresponding locations.

Color Key
- ■ MC
- ▨ CC1
- ▨ CC2
- ▨ CC3
- ■ CC4

greenie Diaper Cover

With the popularity of cloth diapers on the rise, this basic diaper cover makes a very handy gift for earth-friendly parents. The stitch pattern stretches to fit over all cloth diapers, whether they are traditional cloth or the handy fitted ones. Of course, if you prefer to use the regular disposable diapers, this diaper cover will still provide an adorable cover-up, so make a few to match your favorite outfits for junior.

Equipment

YARN: Dk weight (#3 Light).

Shown: Lion Brand, LB Collection Superwash Merino (100% superwash merino; 306 yd [279.8]/3.5 oz [100 g]): #486-108 denim (MC), 1 (1, 1) ball; #486-114 cayenne (CC), 1 (1, 1) ball.

HOOK: H/8 (5.00 mm) or hook needed to obtain gauge.

NOTIONS: Tapestry needle for weaving in ends; lanolin.

Gauge

19 sts by 24 rows = 4"x 4" (10 × 10 cm).

Finished Size

Small (Medium, Large) is sized to fit 6 (12, 18) mths. Diaper cover shown is a size Small (6 mths).

Finished waist: 13½ (15, 16½)" (34.5 [38, 42] cm).

Finished Length: 6½ (7, 8)" (16.5 [18, 20.5] cm).

The Plans

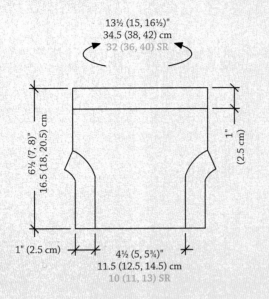

13½ (15, 16½)"
34.5 (38, 42) cm
32 (36, 40) SR

6½ (7, 8)"
16.5 (18, 20.5) cm

1" (2.5 cm)

4½ (5, 5¾)"
11.5 (12.5, 14.5) cm
10 (11, 13) SR

1" (2.5 cm)

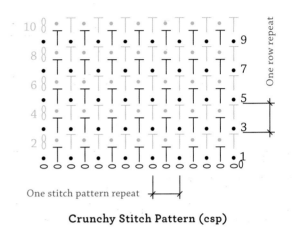

One row repeat

One stitch pattern repeat

Crunchy Stitch Pattern (csp)

Details

CRUNCHY STITCH PATTERN (CSP)

Refer to **Crunchy Stitch Pattern** diagram above right for assistance.

Ch 20.

Row 1 (RS): Sl st in 2nd ch from hook, *hdc in next ch, sl st in next ch, rep from * across, turn—9 hdc or SR.

Row 2: Ch 2 (counts as hdc), *sl st in next hdc, hdc in next sl st, rep from * across, turn.

Row 3: *Sl st in next hdc, hdc in next sl st, rep from * across to end, sl st in top of tch, turn.

Rep Rows 2–3 to desired length.

Construction

DIAPER

See **Stitch Diagram A** on page 103 for assistance.

Ch 65 (73, 81) with MC.

Rnd 1 (RS): Sl st in 2nd ch from hook, *hdc in next ch, sl st in next ch, rep from * across to last ch, hdc in last ch, sl st to first sl st, turn—32 (36, 40) hdc or SR.

Rnd 2: Ch 2 (counts as hdc), *sl st in next hdc, hdc in next sl st, rep from * around to last hdc, sl st in last hdc, sl st to top of tch, turn.

Rnd 3: *Hdc in next sl st, sl st in next hdc, rep from * across to last sl st, hdc in last sl st, sl st in top of first sl st, turn.

Rep Rnds 2–3 four (five, six) more times, turn.

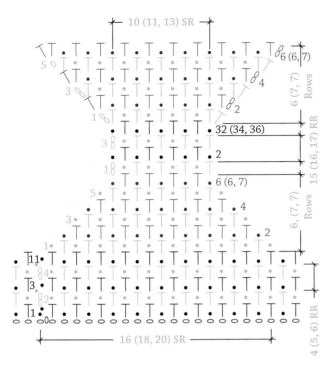

A. Diaper Shaping

DECREASE

Row 1 (WS): Sl st in first hdc, *hdc in next sl st, sl st in next hdc, rep from * 14 (16, 18) more times, turn, leaving rem sts unworked—15 (17, 19) hdc or SR.

Row 2: Sl st in first hdc, *hdc in next sl st, sl st in next hdc, rep from * across to last hdc, turn, leaving rem sl st unworked—14 (16, 18) hdc or SR.
Rep Row 2 four (four, five) more times—10 (11, 13) hdc or SR.

CROTCH

Rep Rows 2–3 of CSP for 32 (36, 40) rows. See Stitch Diagram A above for assistance.

INCREASE

Row 1 (WS): Ch 2 (counts as hdc), hdc in first sl st, *sl st in next hdc, hdc in next sl st, rep from * across to last sl st, hdc in last sl st, turn.

Row 2: Ch 2 (counts as hdc), hdc in first hdc, *sl st in next hdc, hdc in next sl st, rep across to last st, 2 hdc in top of tch, turn.
Rep Row 2 four (four, five) times—16 (17, 20) hdc or SR.
Fasten off, leaving long tail for sewing.

Finishing

Fold diaper in half and pin to last rnd of body of diaper with wrong sides facing. Using long tail, whipstitch edge across. Weave in ends and fasten off.

RIBBING

Join CC to back of diaper with sl st. Ch 5.

Row 1: Sc in 2nd ch from hook and ea ch across, sl st in next 2 sts of body (first sl st joins ribbing to body, second counts as a tch), turn—4 sc.

Row 2: Sk sl sts, sc-blp in each sc across, turn.

Row 3: Ch 1, sc-blp in ea sc across, sl st in next 2 sts of body, turn.
Rep Rows 2–3 evenly around body, fasten off, leaving long tail for seaming.
With tapestry needle, whipstitch ribbing seams together.
Rep Ribbing around both leg openings.

If using as a cloth diaper cover, follow manufacturer's directions to soak diaper cover in lanolin before first use.

andy Cap

How much do we obsess over keeping a baby's head warm while wrestling the little one into a hat? This cap will keep little heads toasty while the baseball cap-style brim keeps sun or rain off the face, without slipping down over baby's eyes. Meanwhile, parents and observers will delight in the funky style of this must-have accessory.

Equipment

YARN: Worsted weight (#4 Medium).

Shown: Caron, Simply Soft Eco (80% acrylic, 20% NatureSpun post-consumer recycled polyester; 249 yd [227 m]/5 oz [142 g]): #0017 spring moss (MC), 1 skein. Caron, Simply Soft (100% acrylic; 157 yd [143 m]/3 oz [85 g]): #2604 bone (CC), 1 skein.

HOOK: I/9 (5.50 mm) and H/8 (5.00 mm) or hooks needed to obtain gauge.

NOTIONS: Tapestry needle for weaving in ends; lightweight cardboard for brim; tracing paper and pencil.

Gauge

16 dc by 12 rows in cap pattern = 4" × 4" (10 × 10 cm).

Finished Size

Small (Medium, Large) cap is sized to fit 16 (18, 19½)" ([40.5, 45.5, 49.5] cm) head circumference. Cap shown is a size Small (16" [40.5 cm] circumference).

Construction

CAP SHAPING

Refer to **Stitch Diagram A** below for assistance.

With MC and I/9 (5.50 mm) hook, make an adjustable ring.

Rnd 1 (RS): Ch 3 (counts as dc), 11 dc in ring, pull ring closed, sl st to top of tch, turn. Cont in Stitch Diagram A for 10 (11, 12) rnds total.

Work even (one st in ea st around) for 6 rnds in the following sequence: one rnd each of *sc, hdc, dc; rep from * once. Do not turn after hdc rnds. Fasten off—66 (72, 78) sts and 16 (17, 18) rnds.

RIBBING

Join CC with H/8 (5.00 mm) hook to back of cap with sl st. Ch 5.

Row 1: Sc in 2nd ch from hook and in ea ch across, sl st in next 2 sts on cap (first sl st joins ribbing to cap, second counts as a tch), turn—4 sc.

Row 2: Sk sl sts, sc-blp in each sc across, turn.

Row 3: Ch 1, sc-blp in ea sc across, sl st in next 2 sts on cap, turn.

Rep Rows 2–3 evenly around cap, fasten off, leaving long tail for seaming.

With tapestry needle, whipstitch ribbing seams together.

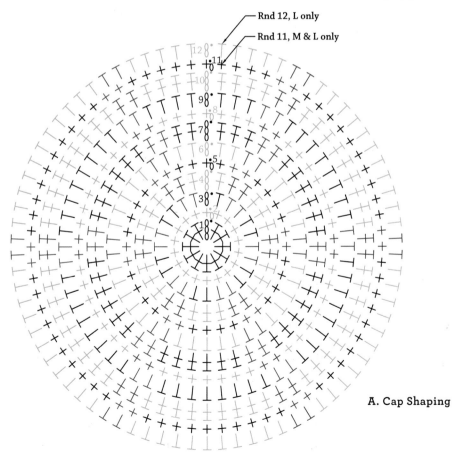

Rnd 12, L only

Rnd 11, M & L only

A. Cap Shaping

Rnd 2: Ch 1, sc in first sc, 2 sc in next sc, sc in next 13 sc, 2 sc in next sc, sc in next sc, 2 sc in next sc, sc in ea sc to last sc, 2 sc in last sc, sl st to first sc, turn—36 sc.

Rnd 3: Ch 1, 2 sc in first sc, sc in next 15 sc, 2 sc in next sc, sc in next sc, 2 sc in next sc, sc in ea sc to last 2 sc, 2 sc in next sc, sc in last sc, sl st to first sc, turn—40 sc.

Rnd 4: Ch 1, sc in first sc, 2 sc in next sc, sc in next 17 sc, 2 sc in next sc, sc in next sc, 2 sc in next sc, sc in ea sc to last sc, 2 sc in last sc, sl st to first sc, turn—44 sc.

Rnd 5: Ch 1, 2 sc in first sc, sc in next 19 sc, 2 sc in next sc, sc in next sc, 2 sc in next sc, sc in ea sc to last 2 sc, 2 sc in next sc, sc in last sc, sl st to first sc, turn—48 sc.

Rnd 6: Ch 1, sc in ea sc around, sl st to first sc, turn.
Rep Rnd 6 three more times, fasten off.

BRIM

See **Stitch Diagram B** below for assistance.

Ch 16 with CC and H/8 hook.

Rnd 1 (RS): Sc in 2nd ch from hook, sc in ea ch across to last ch, 3 sc in last ch, turn work 180 degrees and beg working in free lps of foundation ch, sc in ea ch across to 2nd ch, 2 sc in 2nd ch, sl st to first sc, turn—32 sc.

BRIM SHAPING:

See **Stitch Diagram C** below for assistance.

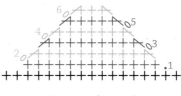

C. Brim Shaping

With RS facing, join CC with sl st in 7 sts to the right of fastening off.

Row 1: Sc in next 13 sc, turn.

Row 2: Ch 1, sc2tog over first 2 sc, sc in ea sc across to last 2 sc, sc2tog over last 2 sc, turn—11 sc.
Rep Row 2 four more times, fasten off.
With RS facing, join CC with sl st 10 sts from end of Row 1, rep shaping on this side, fasten off.

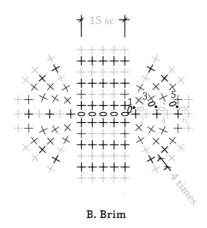

B. Brim

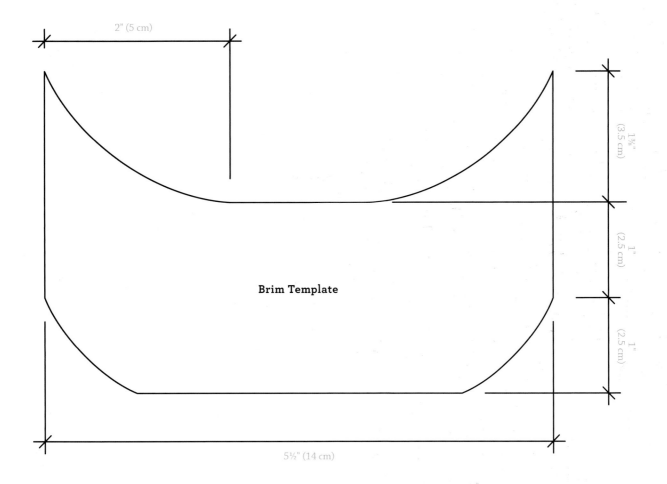

2" (5 cm)

1⅜" (3.5 cm)

1" (2.5 cm)

1" (2.5 cm)

Brim Template

5½" (14 cm)

Finishing

Trim Rnd: Hold CC on WS of fabric, and insert hook (from RS to WS) on any st on Rnd 2 of cap and pull up a lp to RS. Insert hook into next st, following Rnd 2, yo, pull up a lp to RS and through lp on hook (sl st on top of fabric created). Cont around Rnd 2 to first sl st. Fasten off, weave in ends. Rep Trim Rnd on Rnds 3, 8, 9, 14, and 15.

Trace the Brim template above onto tracing paper and cut out. Then transfer the shape to lightweight cardboard with a pencil and cut out. Insert into brim. Join CC to edge of brim. Using H/8 hook, sc around open edge of brim, going through both sides of brim at once to close opening, securing the cardboard. Pin brim to Rnd 16 of cap. Using MC, sew brim to cap with backstitch.

For the Home

Blankets and toys are where you can let your silly side come out to play. I can't think of a better joy than when you hand over a newly crocheted toy and your baby squeals in delight, immediately trying to eat it. Or, when a parent calls you up and says, "Do you think you can teach me to make those bibs? We use them all the time." I just love the pure delight that comes from giving a gift that is truly loved. The projects in this chapter were all designed to be used and loved, whether around the house or around town. Plus, you get the benefit of stretching your wings on even more fun symbol crochet diagrams.

upcycled Washcloth

Washcloths can be a parent's best friend for all of the messes their little ones tend to make. This washcloth is perfect for anything from bath time to washing the dishes. It will hold up to repeated use and will get softer as time goes by. Plus, the machine-washable yarn is made from recycled cotton remnants, making this washcloth an all-around earth-friendly (and convenient) choice for all of your scrubbing needs.

Equipment

YARN: Worsted weight (#4 Medium).

Shown: Lion Brand Yarn, Recycled Cotton Yarn (74% recycled cotton, 24% acrylic, 2% other fiber; 185 yd [169 m]/3.5 oz [100 g]): #482-157 sunshine, 1 ball or #482-124 seashells, 1 ball.

HOOK: H/8 (5.00 mm) or hook needed to obtain gauge.

NOTIONS: Tapestry needle for weaving in ends; stitch markers.

Gauge

18 sts by 18 rows = 4" × 4" (10 × 10 cm) in washcloth stitch pattern.

Finished Size

6" × 6" (15 × 15 cm).

Details

SINGLE CROCHET IN THE MIDDLE BAR: Insert hook into the middle of the wrong side of the hdc stitch, which is formed by the yarnover in the hdc stitch and sc in that loop. The middle bar is below the top loops.

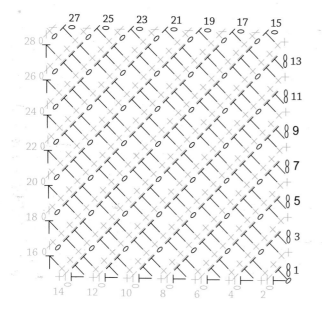

Washcloth Stitch Pattern

Construction

BODY

See **Washcloth Stitch Pattern** diagram at left for assistance.

Ch 3.

Row 1 (RS): 2 hdc in 3rd ch from hook (sk ch count as hdc), turn—3 hdc.

Row 2: Ch 1, 2 sc in middle bar of first hdc, sc in middle bar of next hdc, 2 sc in top of tch, turn—5 sc.

Row 3: Ch 2 (count as hdc), hdc in first sc, hdc in next sc, ch 1, sk next sc, hdc in next sc, 2 hdc in last sc, turn—6 hdc.

Row 4: Ch 1, 2 sc in middle bar of first hdc, sc in middle bar of ea hdc across, sc in ea ch-1 sp across, 2 sc in top of tch, turn—9 sc.

Row 5: Ch 2 (count as hdc), hdc in first sc, hdc in next sc, *ch 1, sk next sc, hdc in next 3 sc, rep from * across to last 3 sc, ch 1, sk next sc, hdc in next sc, 2 hdc in last sc, turn— 9 hdc.

Rep Rows 4–5 four times. Rep Row 4 once—29 sc.

Row 15: Ch 1, sk first sc, hdc in next sc, *ch 1, sk next sc, hdc in next 3 sc, rep from * across to last 3 sc, ch 1, sk next sc, hdc2tog over last 2 sc, turn—20 hdc.

Row 16: Ch 1, sc2tog over hdc2tog and ch-1 sp, sc in middle bar of ea hdc to last hdc, sc in ea ch-1 sp across to last ch-1 sp, sc2tog over last ch-1 sp and last hdc, turn—25 sc.

Rep Rows 15–16 five times.

Row 27: Ch 1, sk first sc, hdc in next sc, ch 1, sk next sc, hdc2tog over last 2 sc, turn—2 hdc.

Row 28: Ch 1, sc3tog over (hdc2tog, ch-1 sp, hdc), fasten off, weave in ends.

EDGING

Attach yarn to RS edge with sl st at corner.

Rnd 1: Ch 1, sc around washcloth evenly, working 3 sc in ea
corner, sl st to first sc, do not turn.

Rnd 2: Rep Rnd 1.

Rnd 3: Ch 1, rev sc in ea sc around to beg, ch 12, sl st to first
sc, fasten off, weave in ends.

burp cloth Bib

Some things a new parent can never have enough of are bibs and burp cloths. This project gives you both of those things in one! The stitch pattern is thick enough to catch any spit-ups from baby food, yet soft enough for baby to bury into when needing to be burped. The strap can be used to secure the bib on a squirmy baby, or it can be fastened around the strap of the diaper bag for easy access. Make several in bright, fun colors so you'll always have one on hand.

Equipment

YARN: DK weight (#3 Light).

Shown: Tahki/Stacy Charles, Cotton Classic (100% mercerized cotton; 108 yd [100 m]/1¾ oz [50 g]):

Option 1 (shown on page 119): #3541 light cantaloupe (MC), 1 hank; #3856 deep indigo (CC1), 1 hank; 3424 deep red (CC2), 1 hank.

Option 2 (shown on page 116): #3456 bright raspberry (MC), 1 hank.

HOOK: H/8 (5.00 mm) or hook needed to obtain gauge.

NOTIONS: Tapestry needle for weaving in ends; stitch markers; spray bottle with water and straight pins for blocking; 1" (2.5 cm) button.

Gauge

21 sts (10 SR) by 26 rows (13 RR) in Woven Stitch Pattern (wsp) = 4" × 4" (10 × 10 cm).

Finished Size

7½" (19 cm) wide by 7" (18 cm) long, excluding strap.

Details

SINGLE CROCHET SPIKE (SC SPIKE): Insert hook into the stitch indicated one row below, skipping over the ch-1 sp, yo, pull up a loop, yo, pull through all loops on the hook.

WOVEN STITCH PATTERN (WSP)

See **Woven Stitch Pattern** diagram below for assistance.

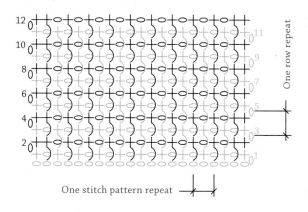

Woven Stitch Pattern (wsp)

✽ **NOTE:** Crochet body and edging of bib then decide on either striped strap (Option 1) or lacy strap (Option 2). The bodies of the two options are identical (just created in different color schemes).

Ch 22.

Row 1 (WS): Sc in 2nd ch from hook, *ch 1, sk 1 ch, sc in next sc, rep from * across to end, turn—11 sc.

Row 2: Ch 1, sc in first sc, *sc spike in next ch on foundation ch, ch 1, sk next sc, rep from * across to last 2 sts, sc spike in next ch on foundation ch, sc in last sc, turn.

Row 3: Ch 1, sc in first sc, *ch 1, sk next sc, sc spike in next sc one row below, rep from * across to last 2 sts, ch 1, sk next sc, sc in last sc, turn.

Row 4: Ch 1, sc in first sc, *sc spike in next sc one row below, ch 1, sk next sc, rep from * across to last 2 sts, sc spike in next sc on row below, sc in last sc, turn.

Rep Rows 3–4 for pattern.

Construction

BODY

See **Stitch Diagram A** below for assistance.

With MC, ch 26.

Row 1 (WS): Sc in 2nd ch from hook, ch 1, sk next ch, sc in next ch, ch 1, sk next ch, (sc, ch 1, sc) in next ch, pm in

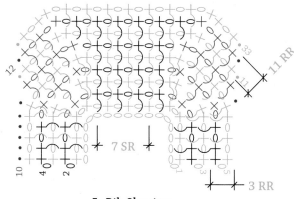

A. Bib Shaping

ch-1 sp, cont in Row 1 of wsp for 7 sc, ch 1, sk next ch, (sc, ch 1, sc) in next ch, pm in ch-1 sp, ch 1, sk next ch, sc in next ch, ch 1, sk next ch, sc in last ch, turn—15 sc.

Row 2: Ch 1, sc in first sc, cont in Row 2 of wsp to m, pm in ch-sp, sc in marked ch-1 sp, ch 1, pm, cont in Row 2 of wsp to m, pm in ch-sp, sc in marked ch-1 sp, ch 1, pm, cont in Row 2 of wsp across to end, turn—16 sc.

Row 3: Cont in Row 3 of wsp to m, 2 sc spike in next sc one row below, pm in first sc, ch 1, 2 sc spike in next sc one row below, pm in second sc, cont in Row 3 of wsp to marker, 2 sc spike in next sc one row below, pm in first sc, ch 1, 2 sc spike in next sc one row below, pm in second sc, cont in Row 3 of wsp to end, turn—19 sc.

Row 4: *Cont in Row 4 of wsp to m, (ch 1, sc) in sc, pm in ch-sp, cont in Row 4 of wsp to m, (sc, ch 1) in sc, pm in ch-sp, rep from * once, cont in Row 4 of wsp to end—20 sc.

Row 5: *Cont in Row 3 of wsp to m, 2 sc spike in next sc one row below, pm in first sc, cont in Row 3 of wsp to m, 2 sc spike in next sc one row below, pm in second sc, rep from * once, cont in Row 3 of wsp to end, turn—23 sc.

Rep Rows 4–5 twice—27 sc.

Row 10: Sl st in next 6 sts, sc spike in next sc one row below, cont in Row 4 of wsp to 1 sc before m, (ch 1, sc) in next sc, cont in Row 4 of wsp to 1 sc past m, (sc, ch 1) in next sc, cont in Row 4 of wsp to last ch-1 before m, sl st in next sc, turn—16 sc.

Row 11: Sk sl st, sl st in next sc, cont in Row 3 of wsp to m, 2 sc in next ch-1 sp, pm in first sc, cont in Row 3 of wsp to m, 2 sc in next ch-1 sp, pm in second sc, cont in Row 3 of wsp to last ch-1, sl st in last sc, turn—17 sc.

Row 12: Sk sl st, sl st in next sc, cont in Row 4 of wsp to m, (ch 1, sc) in next sc, pm in ch-sp, cont in Row 4 of wsp to m, (sc, ch 1) in next sc, cont in Row 4 of wsp to last ch-1 sp, sl st in last sc, turn—16 sc.

Rep Rows 11–12 ten times. Rep Row 11 once, fasten off, weave in ends.

EDGING

Join MC at RS of top of bib with sl st, sc evenly around bib, place 2 sc on outside corners of top of bib, sk 1 st on inside corners of neck, sl st to first sc, fasten off, weave in ends.

STRAP (OPTION 1)

See **Stitch Diagram B** at right for assistance.

Join MC to bib RS at center sc of left top edge.

Row 1: Ch 47, hdc in 8th ch from hook and in ea ch across, sl st to bib, fasten off MC, turn—40 hdc.

Row 2: Join CC1 with sl st to next sc on bib, sk sl st, sc in ea hdc across to ch-7 sp, 14 sc in ch-7 sp, turn work 180 degrees, sc in ea ch across, sl st to bib in next 3 sc, turn—94 sc.

Row 3: Sk sl sts, dc in ea sc across, sl st to bib, turn, fasten off CC1.

Row 4: Join CC2, sl st in ea dc across, fasten off CC2, weave in ends.

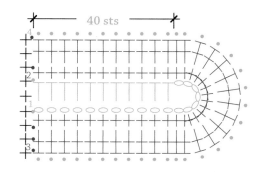

B. Strap Option 1

STRAP (OPTION 2)

See **Stitch Diagram C** below for assistance.

With MC, ch 50, join to bib RS at center sc of left top edge.

Row 1: Sl st in ea ch across to last ch, 3 sl st in last ch, turn work 180 degrees (now work in opposite side of ch), sl st in ea ch across, turn—101 sl st.

Row 2: Ch 1, sl st in next sc on bib edging, sc in next 2 sl sts, *ch 3, sk 2 sl sts, sc in next sl st, ch 2, sk 2 sl sts, sc in next sl st, rep from * across 7 times, ch 6, sk 1 sl st, **sc in next sl st, ch 2, sk 2 sl st, sc in next sl st, ch 3, sk 2 sl st, rep from ** across, sc in last 2 sl sts, sl st to next sc on bib edging, turn—16 ch-3 sps.

Row 3: Sl st in next 2 sc of bib edging, (4dc-cl, ch 4, 4dc-cl) in next and ea ch-3 sp across to ch-6 sp, ([4dc-cl, ch 4] 3 times, 4dc-cl) in ch-6 sp, (4dc-cl, ch 4, 4dc-cl) in next and ea ch-3 sp across, sl st to bib edging, turn—19 ch-4 sps.

Row 4: Sl st in next sc of bib edging, ([sc, ch 3] 4 times, sc) in next and ea ch-4 sp across, sl st to bib edging, fasten off, weave in ends—76 ch-3 sps.

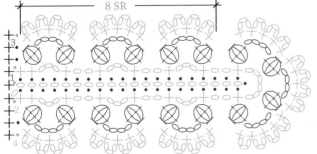

C. Strap Option 2

Finishing

Pin bib to finished size, spray with water, and allow to dry. With MC and tapestry needle, sew button to top right-hand corner of bib.

kyla mod
Stroller Blanket

Aren't granny squares the best? They are so quick to make and are easily portable. This blanket takes the joy of crocheting granny squares and combines it with a modern layout. The resulting bright and pretty blanket mixes fabric textures from lacy to bumpy to provide your little pumpkin with both visual and tactile stimulation. The handy ties included make it easy to attach the blanket securely to your stroller so you can get up and go in style!

Equipment

YARN: Worsted weight (#4 Medium). *Shown:* Blue Sky Alpacas, Worsted Cotton (100% organic cotton; 150 yd [137 m]/1¾ oz [50 g]): #608 lemonade (MC), 3 hanks; #601 poppy (CC1), 1 hank; #617 lotus (CC2), 1 hank; #637 raspberry (CC3), 2 hanks.

HOOK: I/9 (5.50 mm) or hook needed to obtain gauge.

NOTIONS: Spray bottle with water and straight pins for blocking; tapestry needle for weaving in ends.

Gauge

Diamond Star Granny Motif = 6" (15 cm) square.

3 sh by 8 rows (3 SR by 2 RR)= 6" × 3" (15 × 7.5 cm) in Trefoil SP.

2 trefoil and v-sts by 5 rows (2 SR by 2½ RR)= 5" × 3" (12.5 × 7.5 cm) in Lattice SP.

Finished Size

27" × 33" (68.5 × 84 cm).

The Plans

Layout Plan

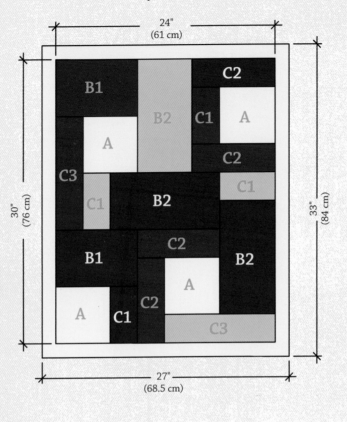

24"
(61 cm)

33"
(84 cm)

30"
(76 cm)

27"
(68.5 cm)

B1, C2, B2, C1, A, C2, A, C3, C1, B2, C1, B1, C2, B2, A, A, C2, C3

Color Legend

- MC
- CC1
- CC2
- CC3

Block Legend

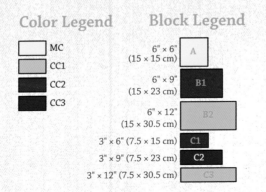

6" × 6" (15 × 15 cm) A

6" × 9" (15 × 23 cm) B1

6" × 12" (15 × 30.5 cm) B2

3" × 6" (7.5 × 15 cm) C1

3" × 9" (7.5 × 23 cm) C2

3" × 12" (7.5 × 30.5 cm) C3

Details

SHELL (SH): (3hdc-cl, ch 2, 3hdc-cl, ch 2,
3hdc-cl, ch 1) in st indicated.
HALF SHELL (HALF SH): (3hdc-cl, ch 2, 2hdc-cl)
in st indicated.
V-ST: (Dc, ch 1, dc) in st indicated.
TREFOIL: (Ch 3, [sc, ch 4] 3 times, sc, ch 3)
in st indicated.

Construction

DIAMOND STAR GRANNY MOTIF
(MAKE 4)

See **Stitch Diagram A** below for assistance.

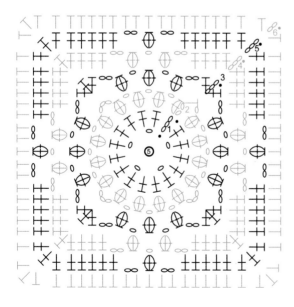

A. Diamond Star Motif

With MC, ch 5, sl st to first ch to form ring.

Rnd 1 (RS): Ch 3 (counts as dc), dc in ring 15 times, sl st in
top of tch, do not turn—16 dc.

Rnd 2: Ch 2, 2dc-cl in top of tch, ch 1, [3dc-cl in next dc, ch
1] twice, 3dc-cl in next dc, ch 3, *[3dc-cl in next dc, ch 1] 3
times, 3dc-cl in next dc, ch 3, rep from * around to last dc,
3 dc-cl in last dc, ch 1, hdc in top of 2dc-cl, do not turn—
fifteen 3dc-cl + one 2 dc-cl.

Rnd 3: Ch 3 (counts as dc), dc in joining hdc, ch 2, [3dc-cl in
next ch-1 sp, ch 1] twice, 3dc-cl in next ch-1 sp, ch 2, *3 dc
in ch-3 sp, ch 2, [3dc-cl in next ch-1 sp, ch 1] twice, 3dc-cl
in next ch-1 sp, ch 2, rep from * around to end, dc in joining hdc, sl st in top of tch, do not turn—twelve 3dc-cl.

Rnd 4: Ch 3 (counts as dc), 2 dc in top of tch, dc in next dc,
dc in ch-2 sp, ch 2, 3dc-cl in next ch-1 sp, ch 1, 3 dc-cl in
next ch-1 sp, ch 2, *dc in ch-2 sp, dc in next dc, 5 dc in next
dc, dc in next dc, dc in ch-2 sp, ch 2, 3dc-cl in next ch-1 sp,
ch 1, 3dc-cl in next ch-1 sp, ch 2, rep from * around, dc in
ch-2 sp, dc in next dc, 2 dc in top of tch of last rnd, sl st in
top of tch, do not turn—36 dc.

Rnd 5: Ch 3 (counts as dc), dc in top of tch, dc in next 4
dc, dc in ch-2 sp, ch 2, 3dc-cl in next ch-1 sp, ch 2, *dc in
ch-2 sp, dc in next 4 dc, 3 dc in next dc, dc in next 4 dc,
dc in ch-2 sp, ch 2, 3dc-cl in next ch-1 sp, ch 2, rep from
* around, dc in ch-2 sp, dc in next 4 dc, dc in top of tch of
last rnd, sl st in top of tch, do not turn—52 dc.

Rnd 6: Ch 2 (counts as hdc), hdc in top of tch, hdc in next 6
dc, 2 hdc in ch-2 sp, hdc in 3dc-cl, 2 hdc in ch-2 sp, hdc in
next 6 dc, *3 hdc in next dc, hdc in next 6 dc, 2 hdc in ch-2
sp, hdc in 3dc-cl, 2 hdc in ch-2 sp, hdc in next 6 dc, rep
from * around, hdc in top of tch of last rnd, sl st in top of
tch, fasten off, weave in ends—80 hdc.

LATTICE STITCH PATTERN BLOCK

Follow **Stitch Diagram B** below.

Note: Instructions are given for 6" × 9" (15 × 23 cm) block and then changes for (6" × 12" [15 × 30.5 cm]) block are in parentheses.

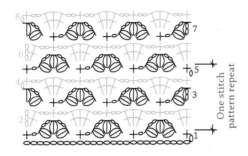

B. Lattice Stitch Pattern

Make one 6" × 9" [15 × 23 cm] each with CC2 and CC3 (make one 6" × 12" [15 × 30.5 cm] block with CC1, make two 6" × 12" [15 × 30.5 cm] with CC3).

Row 1 is the RS.

Crochet 24 rows for a 6" × 9" (15 × 23 cm) block (32 rows for a 6" × 12" [15 × 30.5 cm] block), do not fasten off, turn.

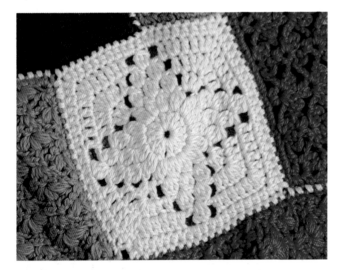

Last Rnd (RS): Ch 1, sc in sc, *sc in ch-sp, sc in next 3 dc, sc in ch-sp, sc in sc, rep from * across, 3 sc in last sc, turn 90 degrees, work 27 (37) sc evenly spaced down side of block, 3 sc at end of side, turn work 90 degrees, work 17 sc across foundation ch to last ch, 3 sc in last ch, turn 90 degrees, work 27 (37) sc evenly spaced up edge of block, 2 sc in last sc, sl st to first sc, fasten off.

TREFOIL STITCH PATTERN BLOCK

See **Stitch Diagram C** below for assistance.

Note: Instructions are given for 3" × 6" (7.5 × 15 cm) block and then changes for (3" × 9" [7.5 × 23 cm], 3" × 12" [7.5 × 30.5 cm]) block are in parentheses.

Make four 3" × 6" (7.5 × 15 cm) blocks: 2 in CC1, 1 in CC2, 1 in CC3 (make four 3" × 9" [7.5 × 23 cm] blocks: 3 in CC2 and 1 in CC3, make one 3" × 12" [7.5 × 30.5 cm] block each with CC1 and CC2).

Ch 30 (40, 50).

Row 1 (RS): Dc in 5th ch from hook, *sk 4 ch, trefoil in next ch, sk 4 ch, v-st in next ch, rep from * once (twice, three) times, sk 4 ch, ch 3, (sc, ch 4, sc, ch 2, dc) in last ch, turn—2 (3, 4) v-sts.

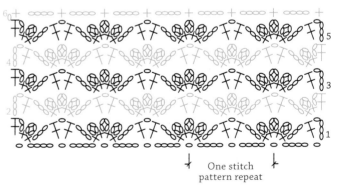

C. Trefoil Stitch Pattern

Finishing

BLOCKING

Pin blocks to schematic sizes. Spray with water and allow to dry.

JOINING

Using layout plan (see THE PLANS on page 124) as guide, pin blocks together with RS facing. With MC, sc across edge of blocks going through both blocks' sts at the same time. Connect all blocks together in the same manner.

EDGING

Rnd 1: With RS facing, join MC to any corner of blanket with sl st. Ch 3 (counts as dc), dc in ea side st around, working 5 dc in each corner, sl st in top of tch, do not turn.

Rnd 2: Ch 3 (counts as dc), dc in ea side st around, working 5 dc in each corner, sl st in top of tch, do not turn.
Rep Rnd 2, fasten off, weave in ends.

TIES

Place a marker 12" (30.5 cm) from each end of blanket on long side edge. *With MC, ch 30, sl st long side edge at marker, ch 31, turn. Sc in 2nd ch from hook and ea ch and sl st across, fasten off. Rep from * 3 more times to create the rem ties.

Row 2: Ch 4 (counts as dc, ch-1 sp), dc in ch-2 sp, *trefoil in next ch-1 sp, sk next ch-4 sp, v-st in next ch-4 sp, rep from * to last trefoil, ch 3, (sc, ch 4, sc, ch 2, dc) in 3rd ch of tch, turn.
Rep Row 2 three times.

Row 6: Ch 1, sc in dc, *ch 4, sc in next ch-1 sp, ch 4, sk next ch-4 sp, sc in next ch-4 sp, rep from * across to last trefoil, ch 4, sc in 3rd ch of tch, turn.

Last Rnd: Ch 1, sc in sc, 17 (27, 37) sc evenly across to last sc, 3 sc in last sc, turn work 90 degrees, work 7 sc evenly space down edge, 3 sc in first foundation ch, work 17 (27, 37) sc evenly spaced across foundation ch to last ch, 3 sc in last ch, turn work 90 degrees, work 7 sc evenly spaced up edge, 2 sc in last st, sl st to first sc, fasten off.

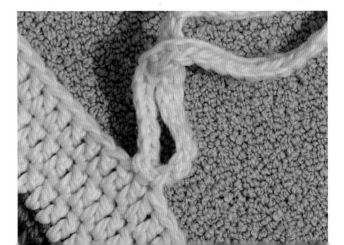

ellie
on Parade

My daughter's favorite animal is definitely the elephant. I don't know whether it's their long trunks, big ears, or chubby bodies, but they make her squeal in delight. So, it was only natural for me to think of elephants when the time came to create a mobile to hang above her crib. This colorful elephant mobile is a delight for my daughter every time she wakes up and sees it. I hope your little peanut enjoys it as much as mine does.

Equipment

YARN: Worsted weight (#4 Medium).

Shown: Tahki/Stacy Charles: Filatura Di Crosa, Zara (100% lana extrafine merino superwash wool; 137 yd [125 m]/1¾ oz [50 g]): #1493 crimson (MC), 2 balls; #1790 mustard (CC1), 1 ball; #1794 coral (CC2), 1 ball; #1798 seafoam green (CC3), 1 ball.

HOOK: G/6 (4.00 mm) or hook needed to obtain gauge.

NOTIONS: Polyester fiberfill; tapestry needle for weaving in ends; 12" (30.5 cm) styrofoam extruded floral craft ring; long sharp needle with eye large enough to accommodate yarn; pliers; hot glue gun and glue sticks.

Gauge

20 sc by 20 rows= 4" × 4" (10 × 10 cm).

Finished Size

Elephant = 3" (7.5 cm) wide by 6" (15 cm) long by 3½" (9 cm) tall.

Mobile = 12" (30.5 cm) in diameter; 8" (20.5 cm) deep.

The Plans

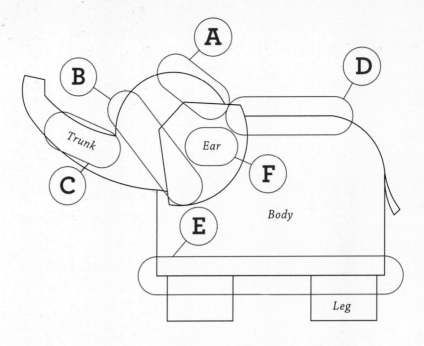

Construction

HEAD (MAKE 1 IN EA COLOR)

See **Stitch Diagram A** at right for assistance.

Head Increase:

Make an adjustable ring, ch 1.

Rnd 1: 6 sc in ring, do not turn.

Rnd 2: 2 sc in ea sc around, do not turn—12 sc.

Rnd 3: *2 sc in next sc, sc in next sc, rep from * around, do not turn—18 sc.

Rnd 4: Sc in next sc, * 2 sc in next sc, sc in next 2 sc, rep

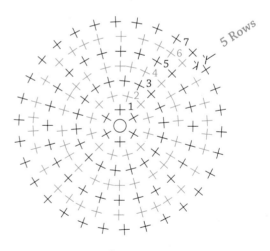

A. Head Increase

from * around to last 2 sc, 2 sc in next sc, sc in last sc, do not turn—24 sc.

Rnd 5: Sc in ea sc around, do not turn.

Rnd 6: *2 sc in next sc, sc in next 3 sc, rep from * around, do not turn—30 sc.

Rnds 7–11: Rep Rnd 5.

Head Decrease:

See **Stitch Diagram B** below for assistance.

Rnd 1: Sc in next sc, *sc2tog over next 2 sc, sc in next 3 sc, rep from * around to last 4 sc, sc2tog over next 2 sc, sc in next 2 sc, do not turn—24 sc.

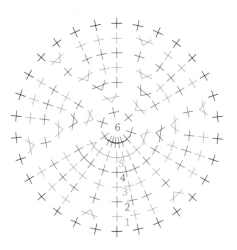

B. Head Decrease

Rnd 2: Sc in ea sc around, do not turn.

Rnd 3: Sc in next 5 sc, *sc2tog over next 2 sc, sc in next 2 sc, rep from * 3 more times, sc in last 3 sc, do not turn—20 sc.

Rnd 4: Sc in next 5 sc, *sc2tog over next 2 sc, sc in next sc, rep from * 3 more times, sc in last 3 sc, do not turn—16 sc.

Rnd 5: Sc in next 3 sc, sc2tog over next 2 sc 5 times, sc in last 3 sc, do not turn—11 sc.

Rnd 6: Sc in ea sc around, do not turn.
Stuff head with fiberfill.

Trunk Decrease:

See **Stitch Diagram C** below for assistance.

Rnd 1: Sc in ea sc around, do not turn.

Rnds 2–4: Sc in next 4 sc, sl st in next 4 sts, sc in last 4 sc, do not turn.

Rnd 5: Sc in next 2 sc, sc2tog over next 2 sc, sc in next 3 sl sts, sc2tog over next 2 sc, sc in last 2 sc, do not turn—9 sc.

Rnd 6: Rep Rnd 1.

Rnd 7: Sc in next 2 sc, sc2tog over next 2 sc, sc in next sc, sc2tog over next 2 sc, sc in last 2 sc, do not turn—7 sc.
Stuff trunk with fiberfill.

Rnds 8–9: Rep Rnd 1.

Rnd 10: Sc2tog over next 2 sc 3 times, sc in last sc, fasten off. Weave end through sts to close trunk.

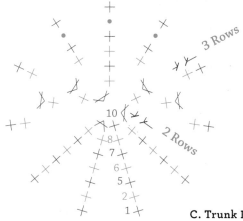

C. Trunk Decrease

BODY (MAKE 1 IN EA COLOR)

Body Increase:

See **Stitch Diagram D** below for assistance.

Ch 10.

Row 1: Sc in 2nd ch from hook, sc in ea ch to last ch, 3 sc in last ch, turn work 180 degrees (now work in opposite side of tch), sc in ea ch across, turn—19 sc.

Row 2: Ch 1, sc in next 8 sc, 2 sc in next 3 sc, sc in ea sc to end, turn—22 sc.

Row 3: Ch 1, sc in next 8 sc, *2 sc in next sc, sc in next sc, rep from * twice more, sc in ea sc across, turn—25 sc.

Row 4: Ch 1, 2 sc in first sc, sc in ea sc across to last sc, 2 sc in last sc, turn—27 sc.

Rows 5–6: Rep Rnd 4—31 sc.

Rnd 7: Ch 1, sc in next 12 sc, *2 sc in next sc, sc in next 2 sc, rep from * twice more, sc in ea sc across, ch 8, sl st in first sc, turn—34 sc.

Rnd 8: Ch 1, sc in next 2 ch, 2 sc in next ch, sc in next 2 ch, 2 sc in next ch, sc in next 2 ch, sc in ea sc around, sl st to first sc, turn—36 sc.

Rnds 9–10: Ch 1, sc in ea sc around, sl st to first sc, turn.

Rnd 11: Ch 1, sc in ea sc around, sl st to first sc, do not turn.

Body Decrease:

See **Stitch Diagram E** below for assistance.

Rnd 1: Sl st in next 4 sc, ch 1, sc in prev sc, turn, ch 4 (leg opening), sk 5 sc, sc in next 2 sc, sc2tog over next 2 sc, sc in next 2 sc, ch 4, sk 5 sc, sc in next 6 sc, ch 4, sk 5 sc, sc in next 2 sc, sc2tog over next 2 sc, sc in next 2 sc, ch 4, sk 5 sc, sc in ea sc to end, sl st to first sc, turn—22 sc.

Rnd 2: Ch 1, sc in next 5 sc, 3 sc in next ch-4 sp, sc in next 2 sc, sk sc2tog, sc in next 2 sc, 3 sc in next ch-4 sp, sc in next 6 sc, 3 sc in next ch-4 sp, sc in next 2 sc, sk sc2tog, sc in next 2 sc, 3 sc in next ch-4 sp, sc in last sc, sl st to first sc, turn—32 sc.

Rnd 3: Ch 1, sc in next 3 sc, [sc2tog over next 2 sc] 3 times, sc in next 10 sc, [sc2tog over next 2 sc] 3 times, sc in next 7 sc, turn—26 sc.

Rnd 4: Ch 1, sc in next 7 sc, sc3tog over next 3 sts, sc in next 10 sc, sc3tog over next 3 sts, sc in ea sc to end, sl st to first sc, fasten off with long tail. Using long tail, whipstitch opening closed—22 sc.

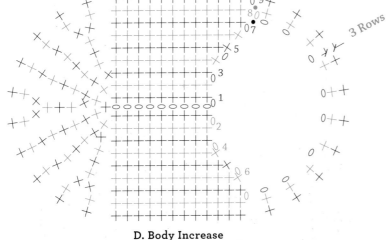

D. Body Increase

E. Body Decrease

LEGS

Rnd 1: Join yarn with sl st to any ch-4 sp, 9 sc evenly spaced around leg opening, do not join, do not turn.

Rnd 2: *2 sc in next sc, sc in next 2 sc, rep from * around, do not turn—12 sc.

Rnds 3–5: Sc in ea sc around, do not turn.

Rnd 6: [Sc2tog-blp over next 2 sc] 6 times, fasten off with long tail, close leg with tail—6 sc.

Stuff body and legs with fiberfill.

Rep Rnds 1–6 on ea of the rem 3 leg openings.

EAR (MAKE 2 IN EA COLOR)

See **Stitch Diagram F** below for assistance.

Ch 6.

Row 1: Sc in 2nd ch from hook, sc in ea ch, turn—5 sc.

Row 2: Ch 1, *2 sc in next sc, sc in next sc, rep from * once, 2 sc in last sc, turn—8 sc.

Row 3: Ch 1, 2 sc in first sc, sc in ea sc to last, 2 sc in last sc, turn—10 sc.

Rows 4–5: Ch 1, sc in ea sc across, turn.

Row 6: Ch 1, sc2tog over first 2 sc, sc in next 2 sc, 2 sc in each of next 2 sc, sc in next 2 sc, sc2tog over last 2 sc, turn work 90 degrees, sc down side of Ear, 2 sc in first ch, sc in ea ch across foundation ch, 2 sc in last ch, sc up side of Ear, fasten off, weave in ends.

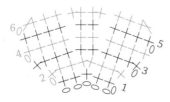

F. Ear

TAIL (MAKE 1 IN EA COLOR)

Ch 4, sl st to Body, sc in ea ch, fasten off.

Finishing

With tapestry needle and leftover yarn, sew Head to Body and Ears to Head. With tapestry needle and contrasting color, embroider eyes and toenails onto elephant with satin stitch. Rep for ea elephant.

Dab a bit of hot glue on the styrofoam ring, lay MC on the glue and begin wrapping yarn around ring, keeping strands close together. Every 3" (7.5 cm) or so, dab a bit of glue on ring and secure yarn as before.

Cut a 7 ft (2.1 m) piece of any yarn and thread through sharp needle. Pierce styrofoam ring (from top to bottom at any point along ring) with sharp needle, grasp needle with pliers, and pull through. Thread half of yarn through ring. Ch 25 above ring, fasten off. Ch 15 below ring, sl st to elephant's body (any color; sample features ea elephant with a contrasting color string) behind the head, fasten off, weave in ends. Rep with ea elephant so that all elephants hang from the bottom of the ring and are equally spaced. Holding all the 25-ch strings, tie a knot at center of ring. Then, create a loop with the thread tails and tie another knot to form a hanging loop.

robot
Burt

Burt is the 'bot for every baby. His arms and legs are great for the little grabbers, and his size and soft body are perfect for their budding imaginations. Plus, the simple shapes provide the perfect opportunity for you to practice your sculptural crochet diagram skills. This sweet little 'bot is sure to bring a smile to your little guy or gal!

Equipment

YARN: Worsted weight (#4 Medium).
Shown: Caron, Simply Soft (100% acrylic; 366 yd [334.6 m]/7 oz [198.4 g]): #2628 dark country blue (MC), 1 skein; #9941 persimmon (CC2), 1 skein.
Caron, Simply Soft Eco (80% acrylic, 20% NatureSpun post-consumer recycled polyester; 249 yd [227 m]/5 oz [142 g]): #0027 ocean (CC1), 1 skein; #0012 wine country (CC3), 1 skein.

HOOK: H/8 (5.00 mm) or hook needed to obtain gauge.

NOTIONS: Polyester fiberfill; tapestry needle for weaving in ends; stitch marker.

Gauge

18 sc by 21 rows= 4" × 4" (10 × 10 cm).

Finished Size

Burt is 4" wide × 9" tall (10 × 23 cm), seated.

The Plans

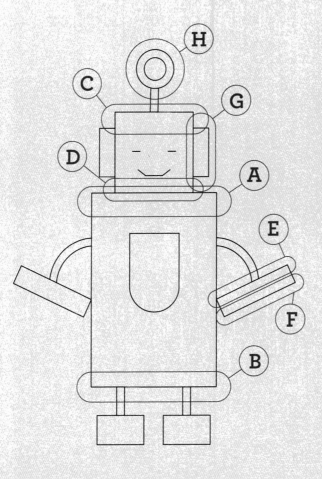

Construction

BODY

Body Increase:

See **Stitch Diagram A** on page 137 for assistance.

Make an adjustable ring with MC.

Rnd 1: Ch 1, 4 sc in ring, pull ring closed, sl st to first sc, do not turn.

Rnd 2: Ch 1, 2 sc in ea sc around, sl st to first sc, do not turn—8 sc.

Rnd 3: Ch 1, sc in first 2 sc, *2 sc in next sc, sc in next sc, rep from * around, sc in first sc of prev rnd, sl st to first sc, do not turn—12 sc.

Rnd 4: Ch 1, sc in first sc, *3 sc in next sc, sc in next 2 sc, rep from * around, sl st to first sc, do not turn—20 sc.

Rnd 5: Ch 1, sc in first 2 sc, *3 sc in next sc, sc in next 4 sc, rep from * around, ending with sc in each of last 2 sc, sl st to first sc, do not turn—28 sc.

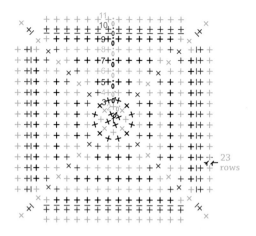

A. Body Increase

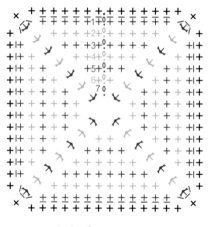

B. Body Decrease

Rnd 6: Ch 1, sc in first 3 sc, *3 sc in next sc, sc in next 6 sc, rep from * around, ending with sc in each of last 3 sc, sl st to first sc, do not turn—36 sc.

Rnd 7: Ch 1, sc in first 4 sc, *3 sc in next sc, sc in next 8 sc, rep from * around, ending with sc in each of last 4 sc, sl st to first sc, do not turn—44 sc.

Rnd 8: Ch 1, sc in first 5 sc, *3 sc in next sc, sc in next 10 sc, rep from * around, ending with sc in each of last 5 sc, sl st to first sc, do not turn—52 sc.

Rnd 9: Ch 1, sc in first 6 sc, *3 sc in next sc, sc in next 12 sc, rep from * around, ending with sc in each of last 6 sc, sl st to first sc, do not turn—60 sc.

Rnd 10: Ch 1, sc-blp in ea sc around, sl st to first sc, do not turn.

Rnd 11: Ch 1, sc in ea sc around, sl st to first sc, do not turn. Rep Rnd 11 twenty-three times.

Body Decrease:

See **Stitch Diagram B** at left for assistance.

Rnd 1: Ch 1, sc-flp in next 6 sc, *sc3tog-flp over next 3 sc, sc-flp in next 12 sc, rep from * around, ending with sc in each of last 6 sc, sl st to first sc, do not turn—52 sc.

Rnd 2: Ch 1, sc in next 5 sc, *sc3tog over next 3 sc, sc in next 10 sc, rep from * around, ending with sc in each of last 5 sc, sl st to first sc, do not turn—44 sc.

Stuff body with fiberfill.

Rnd 3: Ch 1, sc in next 4 sc, *sc3tog over next 3 sc, sc in next 8 sc, rep from * around, ending with sc in each of last 4 sc, sl st to first sc, do not turn—36 sc.

Rnd 4: Ch 1, sc in next 3 sc, *sc3tog over next 3 sc, sc in next 6 sc, rep from * around, ending with sc in each of last 3 sc, sl st to first sc, do not turn—28 sc.

Rnd 5: Ch 1, sc in next 2 sc, *sc3tog over next 3 sc, sc in next 4 sc, rep from * around, ending with sc in each of last 2 sc, sl st to first sc, do not turn—20 sc.

Rnd 6: Ch 1, sc in next sc, *sc3tog over next 3 sc, sc in next 2 sc, rep from * around, ending with sc in last sc, sl st to first sc, do not turn—12 sc.

Rnd 7: Ch 1, *sc3tog over next 3 sc, rep from * around, sl st to first sc, fasten off, weave tail through rnd to close rnd—4 sc.

HEAD

Head Increase:

With CC1, make an adjustable ring, ch 1.

Rnd 1: 8 sc in ring, pull ring closed, sl st to first sc, do not turn.

Follow **Stitch Diagram C** below for 14 rnds total.

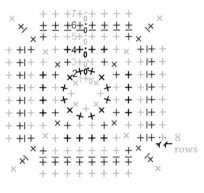

C. Head Increase

Head Decrease:

Follow **Stitch Diagram D** below for 4 rnds. Stuff head with fiberfill after Rnd 1. Fasten off and weave tail through last rnd to close. Sew head to body by connecting the last rnd of the head to the first rnd of the body.

HAND (MAKE 2)

Hand Increase:

With CC2, Make an adjustable ring, Ch 1.

Rnd 1: 6 sc in ring, pull ring closed, sl st to first sc, do not turn.

Follow **Stitch Diagram E** below for 6 rnds total.

Hands Decrease:

Follow **Stitch Diagram F** below for 3 rnds. Stuff hands with fiberfill after Rnd 1. Fasten off and weave tail through last round to close.

ARM (MAKE 2)

With MC, ch 5, sl st in 2nd ch from hook, sl st in ea ch across, turn work 180 degrees, beg working in free lps of chain, sl st in ea ch across, fasten off, leaving long tail for sewing.

Sew Hands to Arms and Arms to Body with tails.

EAR (MAKE 2)

See **Stitch Diagram G** below for assistance. Make an adjustable ring with CC2.

Rnd 1: Ch 1, 8 sc in ring, pull ring closed, sl st to first sc, do not turn.

Rnd 2: Ch 1, 2 sc in ea sc around, sl st to first sc, do not turn—16 sc.

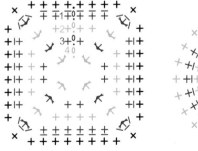

D. Head Decrease

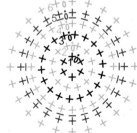

E. Hands Increase

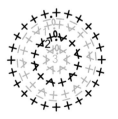

F. Hands Decrease

G. Ear

H. Antenna

Rnd 3: Ch 1, sc-blp in ea sc around, sl st to first sc, fasten off, leaving long tail for sewing.

Stuff ears with fiberfill. Sew one ear to each side of head.

ANTENNA

See **Stitch Diagram H** at left for assistance.

Ch 6 with CC3, sl st to first ch to form ring.

Rnd 1: Ch 1, 14 sc in ring, sl st to first sc, do not turn.

Row 2: Ch 4, sl st in 2nd ch from hook, sl st in ea ch, turn work 180 degrees, beg working in free lps of chain, sl st in next 3 ch, fasten off, leaving long tail for sewing.

With yarn tail and tapestry needle, sew antenna to top of head, centered, as pictured on page 134.

LEG (MAKE 2)

With MC, ch 15, sl st in 2nd ch from hook, sl st in ea ch across, turn work 180 degrees, beg working in free lps of chain, sl st in ea ch across, leaving long tail for sewing.

FOOT (MAKE 2)

Make an adjustable ring with CC3.

Rnd 1: Ch 1, 4 sc in ring, pull ring closed, sl st to first sc, do not turn.

Rnd 2: Ch 1, 3 sc in ea sc around, sl st to first sc, do not turn—12 sc.

Rnd 3: Ch 1, sc-blp in ea sc around, sl st to first sc, do not turn.

Rnd 4: Ch 1, sc in ea sc around, sl st to first sc, do not turn.

Rep Rnd 4 five times.

Stuff feet with fiberfill.

Last Rnd: Ch 1, sc3tog over next 3 sc, rep around, sl st to first sc, fasten off, leaving long tail for sewing.

Sew feet to legs and legs to body.

BREASTPLATE

With CC3, ch 7.

Row 1: Sc in 2nd ch from hook, sc in ea ch across, turn—6 sc.

Row 2: Ch 1, sc in ea sc across, turn.

Rep Row 2 five times.

Row 8: Ch 1, sc2tog over next 2 sc, sc in next 2 sc, sc2tog over last 2 sc, turn—4 sc.

Row 9: Ch 1, [sc2tog over next 2 sc] twice, do not turn.

Last Rnd: Sc evenly around Breastplate, placing 3 sc in each outside corner, sl st to first sc, leaving long tail for sewing.

Sew Breastplate to center front of body with long tail as pictured on page 134.

Finishing

Making sure the face is on the same side as the Breastplate, with tapestry needle and CC3, backstitch smile on head over 4 sc. Embroider eyes on head using a straight stitch over one sc 5 times.

froggie Blanket

When there is a new baby to crochet for, one of the first projects that comes to mind is, of course, a blanket. So, why not use some impressive techniques to highlight your crocheted masterpiece? Tunisian crochet makes up the main portion of this cozy blanket, producing a wonderfully textured fabric that is still light and airy. The cute froggie appliqué can be crocheted easily with the included instructions and stitch diagram and adds a touch of whimsy to this useful piece.

Equipment

YARN: Worsted weight (#4 Medium).

Shown: Red Heart, Eco-Ways (70% acrylic, 30% recycled polyester; 186 yd [170 m]/4 oz [113 g]): #3518 peacock (MC), 3 balls; #3422 yam (CC1), 2 balls; #1615 lichen (CC2), 1 ball.

HOOK: K/10.5 (6.50 mm) afghan hook, I/9 (5.50 mm), and H/8 (5.00 mm) or hooks needed to obtain gauge.

NOTIONS: Tapestry needle for weaving in ends; spray bottle with water and straight pins for blocking; ⅜" (1 cm) button.

Gauge

5 sh by 10 rows (5 SR by 5 RR)= 4" × 3¾" (10 × 9.5 cm) in Ocean Stitch Pattern (osp) with K/10.5 (6.5 mm) hook.

Finished Size

28" × 37" (71 × 94 cm).

The Plans

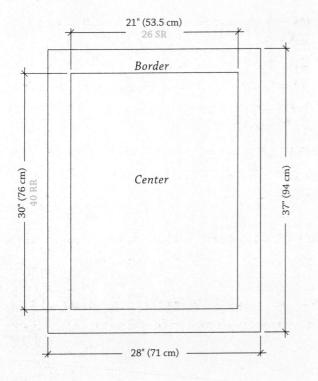

21" (53.5 cm)
26 SR

Border

Center

30" (76 cm)
40 RR

37" (94 cm)

28" (71 cm)

NOTE: See the sidebar on page 145 for an introduction to Tunisian crochet and the Tunisian crochet stitch key.

Row 2 Fwd: Ch 1, sk half sh, *pull up lp in next ch, pull up lp in ch between sh on foundation ch, sk next ch, pull up lp in next ch, sk next sh, rep from * across to end, pull up lp in top of half sh.

Row 2 Ret: Yo, pull through 1 lp on hook, ch 1, *yo, pull through 4 lps on hook, ch 2, rep from * across to last 5 lps on hook, yo, pull through 4 lps on hook, ch 1, pull through last 2 lps on hook—5 sh/SR.

Row 3 Fwd: Ch 1, sk first vertical bar, pull up lp in next ch, *sk next sh, pull up lp in next ch, pull up lp on top of sh 1 row below, sk next ch, pull up lp in next ch, rep from * across to end, sk next sh, pull up lp in next ch, sk next ch, pull up lp in last vertical bar.

OCEAN STITCH PATTERN (OSP)

Refer to **Ocean Stitch Pattern** diagram at right for assistance.

Ch 16 with K/10.5 (6.50 mm) afghan hook.

Row 1 Fwd: Pull up lp in 2nd ch from hook and in ea ch across.

Row 1 Ret: Yo, pull through 2 lps on hook (half sh made), *ch 2, yo, pull through 4 lps on hook (ch 3 and sh made), rep from * across to last 3 lps on hook, ch 2, yo, pull through last 3 lps on hook (half sh made).

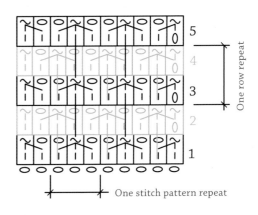

One row repeat

One stitch pattern repeat

Ocean Stitch Pattern (osp)

in top of sh 1 row below, yo, pull through 2 lps on hook, sk next ch, sc in next ch, sk next sh, rep from * across, sk next sh, sc in next ch, sk next ch, sc in last vertical bar, do not turn.

Edging Rnd: Change to I/9 (5.50 mm) hook, ch 1, sc evenly down side, 3 sc in first foundation ch, sc in ea ch across, 3 sc in last ch, sc evenly up side, 3 sc in first sc, sc in ea sc across to last sc, 3 sc in last sc, sl st to first sc, fasten off, weave in ends.

BORDER

With I/9 (5.50 mm) hook and CC1, join yarn to corner of edging on RS.

Follow **Stitch Diagram A** below for 11 rnds. Join each rnd with a sl st to the first st and turn work, fasten off.

With same hook and CC2, join yarn to Rnd 10 with a sl st on top of Border. Sl st around border on Rnd 10 on top of fabric

Row 3 Ret: Yo, pull through 2 lps on hook, *ch 2, yo, pull through 4 lps on hook, rep from * across to last 3 lps on hook, ch 2, yo, pull through last 3 lps on hook.

Row 4 Fwd: Ch 1, sk half sh, *pull up lp in next ch, pull up lp on top of sh 1 row below, sk next ch, pull up lp in next ch, sk next sh, rep from * across to end, pull up lp in top of half sh.

Row 4 Ret: Yo, pull through 1 lp on hook, ch 1, *yo, pull through 4 lps on hook, ch 2, rep from * across to last 5 lps on hook, yo, pull through 4 lps on hook, ch 1, pull through last 2 lps on hook.

Rep Rows 3–4 to desired length.

Construction

CENTER

Ch 79 with MC and K/10.5 (6.50 mm) afghan hook.
Follow directions for osp for 80 rows total—26 sh/SR.

Last Row: Ch 1, sc in next ch, sk sh, *sc in next ch, pull up lp

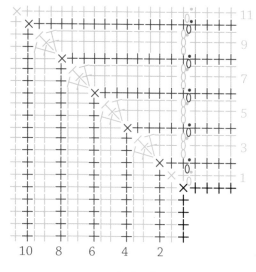

A. Border

(insert hook into rnd from RS to WS and pull up yarn from WS to RS, pull through lp on hook), sl st to first st, fasten off. Rep on Rnd 8.

Finishing

BLOCKING

Pin blanket to schematic size. Spritz with water and allow to dry.

FROGGIE APPLIQUÉ

Follow **Stitch Diagram B** below to crochet froggie body with CC2 and H/8 (5.00 mm) hook for 25 rows, do not turn.

Last Rnd: Sc evenly around entire froggie body, 2 sc in outside corners, sl st to first sc, fasten off, leaving long tail for sewing. Rep with froggie back leg, following **Stitch Diagram C** below.

Last Rnd: Sc evenly around entire back leg, 2 sc in outside corners, sl st to first sc, fasten off, leaving long tail for sewing.

Rep with froggie front leg, following **Stitch Diagram D** below.

Last Rnd: Sl st around long part of front leg and sc around short part of front leg, sl st to first st, fasten off, leaving long tail for sewing.

Using tails, sew froggie body appliqué to lower right-hand corner of blanket. Sew back leg with large end over back end of body, angled to the right. Sew front leg with large end over front of body, extending leg down and to the right (refer to the **Construction Diagram** below). Sew button to froggie head for eye.

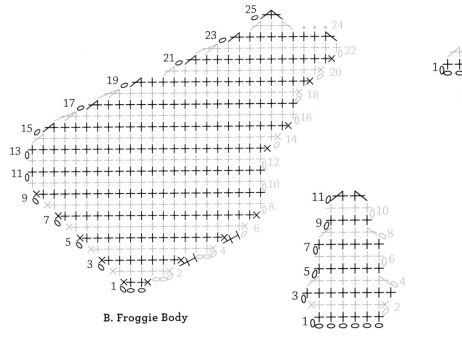

B. Froggie Body

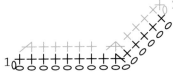

D. Froggie Front Leg

C. Froggie Back Leg

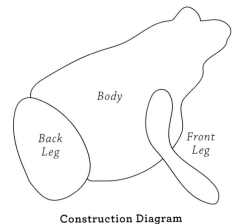

Construction Diagram

Introduction to Tunisian Crochet Symbols

There are several main stitches in Tunisian crochet, but I want to concentrate on the two that you will be working with. The simplest and most common stitch is called the Tunisian Simple Stitch (TSS). First, on the forward pass you insert your hook into the vertical bar of the stitch below, yarn over, and pull up a loop. Then, on the return pass, you yarn over and pull through two loops. The second most common stitch is the Tunisian Purl Stitch (TPS). On the forward pass you bring the yarn to the front of the fabric, insert your hook into the stitch below, yarn over, and draw up a loop. The return pass is worked in the same manner as TSS. Now, let's look at the stitches in symbol form.

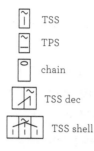

Tunisian Symbols

At top right, you will see a sampling of a few Tunisian stitches. Each stitch is divided into two symbols; one for the forward pass and one for the return. The lower half of the box is the forward pass and the upper half is the return. The TSS forward symbol is a vertical line, which is exactly the same as the fabric you get with TSS, vertical lines. The TPS forward symbol is a horizontal line, which mimics the fabric you get with TPS, horizontal lines. The return symbol for TSS and TPS is a squiggle line representing the "yarn over, pull through two loops" motion.

If we continue looking at the stitch key you will see a symbol that looks like a chain stitch in the return field. And that is exactly what it is: a chain. Sometimes, instead of yarning over and pulling through two loops, the pattern will want you to yarn over and pull through, creating a chain. You usually need to chain when you are making a shell and do not want to decrease the number of stitches in the row.

The last two stitch symbols in the stitch key show the difference between a TSS decrease and a shell. In the decrease stitch you insert your hook into two stitches instead of one on the forward pass and work off like usual. In the shell, you work the forward row as usual and pull through more stitches on the return row. The number of stitches you pull off or pick up is shown in the diagram by each vertical or diagonal line. So, just as regular symbol crochet shows you where to place your hook, Tunisian symbol crochet does the same. The stitch diagrams will feature a different color for each row and the row numbers, just like traditional stitch diagrams do.

Glossary

Abbreviations

beg	begin/beginning	rem	remain(s)/remaining
bet	between	rep	repeat(s)
blp	through back loop(s) only	rev	reverse
CC	contrasting color	rnd	round
ch	chain	RR	row repeat
ch-sp	chain space	RS	right side
cm	centimeter(s)	sc	single crochet
cont	continue	sh	shell
dc	double crochet	sk	skip
dc-cl	double crochet cluster	sl st	slip stitch
dec	decrease/decreases/decreasing	SP	stitch pattern
dtr	double treble crochet	SR	stitch pattern repeat
ea	each	st(s)	stitch(es)
esc	extended single crochet	tch	turning chain
est	established	tog	together
flp	through front loop(s) only	tr	treble crochet
foll	follow/follows/following	WS	wrong side
g	gram(s)	yd	yard(s)
hdc	half double crochet	yo	yarn over
inc	increase/increases/increasing	*	repeat instructions following asterisk as directed
lp(s)	loop(s)	**	repeat all instructions between asterisks as directed
MC	main color	()	alternate instructions and/or measurements
m	marker	[]	work bracketed instructions specified number of times
mth(s)	month(s)		
opp	opposite		
patt	pattern		
pm	place marker		
prev	previous		

Terms

GAUGE

The quickest way to check gauge is to make a square of fabric about 4" × 4" (10 × 10 cm) or motif indicated in pattern for gauge with the suggested hook size and in the indicated stitch. If your measurements match the measurements of the pattern's gauge, congratulations! If you have too many stitches, try going up a hook size; if you have too few stitches, try going down a hook size. Crochet another swatch with the new hook until your gauge matches what is indicated in the pattern.

If the gauge has been measured after blocking, be sure to wet your swatch and block it before taking measurements to check gauge. Wet blocking drastically affects the gauge measurement, especially in lace stitch work.

ROW REPEAT (RR)

The indicated row or rows that are repeated to create a crochet fabric.

STITCH PATTERN REPEAT (SR)

The indicated stitches that are duplicated on the same row to create the stitch pattern.

Crochet Stitches

CROCHET CHAIN (CH)

Make a slipknot and place it on crochet hook. *Yarn over hook and draw through loop on hook. Repeat from * for the desired number of stitches.

SLIP STITCH (SL ST)

*Insert hook into stitch, yarn over hook and draw loop through stitch and loop on hook. Repeat from *.

SINGLE CROCHET (SC)

Insert hook into a stitch, yarn over hook and draw up a loop (*figure 1*), yarn over hook and draw it through both loops on hook (*figure 2*).

Figure 1

Figure 2

Reverse Single Crochet (rev sc)

Insert hook into previous stitch, yarn over hook and draw up a loop, yarn over hook and draw it through both loops on hook. *Rev sc is worked in the opposite direction from sc.*

Extended Single Crochet (esc)

Insert hook into next stitch, yarn over hook and draw up a loop, yarn over hook, draw through 1 loop on hook, yarn over hook, draw through remaining 2 loops on hook.

Single Crochet 2 Together (sc2tog)

Insert hook into indicated stitch, yarn over hook and draw up a loop, insert hook into next stitch, yarn over hook and draw up a loop, yarn over hook, draw through all 3 loops on hook—1 decrease made.

Single Crochet 3 Together (sc3tog)

Insert hook into indicated stitch, yarn over hook, pull up a loop, [insert hook into next stitch, yarn over hook and draw up a loop] twice, yarn over hook, draw through all 4 loops on hook—2 decreases made.

ADJUSTABLE RING

Make a large loop with the yarn *(figure 1)*. Holding the loop with your fingers, insert hook into loop and pull working yarn through loop *(figure 2)*. Yarn over hook, pull through loop on hook.

Continue to work indicated number of stitches into loop *(figure 3; shown in single crochet)*. Pull on yarn tail to close loop *(figure 4)*.

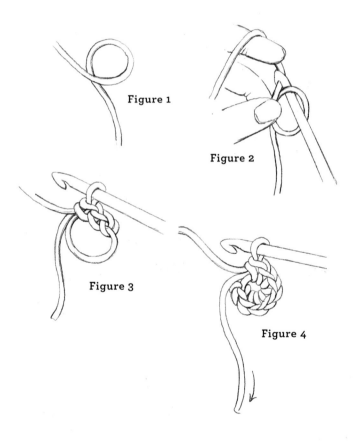

Figure 1

Figure 2

Figure 3

Figure 4

HALF DOUBLE CROCHET (HDC)

*Yarn over hook, insert hook into a stitch, yarn over hook and draw up a loop (3 loops on hook), yarn over hook *(figure 1)* and draw it through all loops on hook *(figure 2)*. Repeat from *.

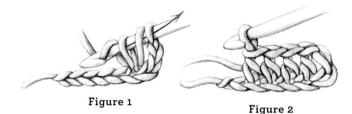

Figure 1

Figure 2

Half Double Crochet 2 Together (hdc2tog)
Yarn over hook, insert hook into indicated stitch, yarn over hook and draw up a loop (3 loops on hook), yarn over hook, insert hook into next stitch, yarn over hook and draw up a loop (5 loops on hook), yarn over hook and draw it through all loops on hook—1 decrease made.

Half Double Crochet 3 Together (hdc3tog)
Yarn over hook, insert hook into indicated stitch, yarn over hook and draw up a loop (3 loops on hook), [yarn over hook, insert hook into next stitch, yarn over hook and draw up a loop] twice (7 loops on hook), yarn over hook and draw through all loops on hook—2 decreases made.

2 Half Double Crochet Cluster (2hdc-cl)
[Yarn over hook, insert hook into indicated stitch, yarn over hook, draw up loop] twice, yarn over hook, draw through all 5 loops on hook.

3 Half Double Crochet Cluster (3hdc-cl)
[Yarn over hook, insert hook into indicated stitch, yarn over hook, draw up loop] 3 times, yarn over hook, draw through all 7 loops on hook.

DOUBLE CROCHET (DC)

*Yarn over hook, insert hook into a stitch, yarn over hook and draw up a loop (3 loops on hook; *figure 1*), yarn over hook and draw it through 2 loops *(figure 2)*, yarn over hook and draw it through remaining 2 loops on hook *(figure 3)*. Repeat from *.

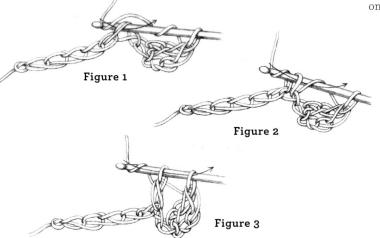

Figure 1

Figure 2

Figure 3

Double Crochet 2 Together (dc2tog)

Yarn over hook, insert hook into next indicated stitch, yarn over hook and draw up a loop, yarn over hook and draw yarn through 2 loops, yarn over hook, insert hook into next indicated stitch and draw up a loop, yarn over hook, draw yarn through 2 loops, yarn over hook and draw yarn through remaining 3 loops on hook—1 decrease made.

2 Double Crochet Cluster (2dc-cl)

[Yarn over hook, insert hook into indicated stitch, yarn over hook, draw up loop, yarn over hook, draw through 2 loops on hook] twice, yarn over hook, draw through remaining 3 loops on hook.

3 Double Crochet Cluster (3dc-cl)

[Yarn over hook, insert hook into indicated stitch, yarn over hook, draw up loop, yarn over hook, draw through 2 loops on hook] 3 times, yarn over hook, draw through remaining 4 loops on hook.

TREBLE CROCHET (TR)

*Wrap yarn around hook twice, insert hook into next indicated stitch, yarn over hook and draw up a loop (4 loops on hook; *figure 1*), yarn over hook and draw it through 2 loops *(figure 2)*, yarn over hook and draw it through the next 2 loops, yarn over hook and draw it through remaining 2 loops on hook *(figure 3)*. Repeat from *.

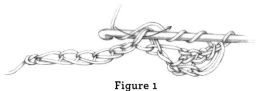

Figure 1

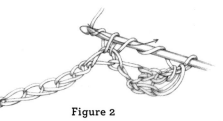

Figure 2

Figure 3

WHIPSTITCH SEAM

With right sides of work facing and working through edge stitches, bring threaded needle out from back to front, along edge of piece.

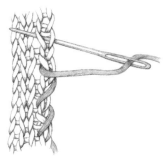

Embroidery Stitches

BACKSTITCH

Working from right to left, bring needle up at 1 and insert behind the starting point at 2. Bring the needle up at 3, repeat by inserting at 1 and bring the needle up at a point that is a stitch length beyond 3.

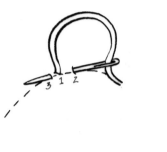 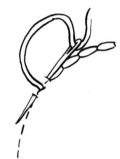

SATIN STITCH

Generally worked from left to right, this stitch is used to fill shapes. Bring the needle up at 1, insert at 2, and bring back up at 3. Repeat.

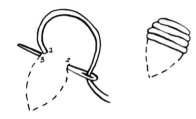

STRAIGHT STITCH

Working from right to left, make a straight stitch by bringing the needle up and then inserting ⅛" to ¼" (3 to 6 mm; or longer as necessary) away from the starting point.

Resources

Blue Sky Alpacas
PO Box 88
Cedar, MN 55011
blueskyalpacas.com
Worsted Cotton

Caron International
PO Box 222
Washington, NC 27889
caron.com
Naturally Caron, Spa
Naturally Caron, Country
Simply Soft
Simply Soft, Eco

Classic Elite
122 Western Avenue
Lowell, MA 01851
classiceliteyarns.com
Pebbles
Summer Sox
Provence

Coats and Clark: Red Heart
PO Box 12229
Greenville, SC 29612
redheart.com
Designer Sport
Eco-Ways

Lion Brand Yarn
135 Kero Road
Carlstadt, NJ 07072
lionbrand.com
LB Collection,
Cotton Bamboo
LB Collection, Superwash
Merino

Spud and Chloë
(a division of
Blue Sky Alpacas)
ATTN: Spud and Chloë
PO Box 88
Cedar, MN 55011
spudandchloe.com
Sweater
Fine

Tahki/ Stacy Charles
70-30 80th St. Bldg. 36
Ridgewood, NY 11385
tahkistacycharles.com
Filatura Di Crosa, Zara
Filatura Di Crosa, Zarina
Cotton Classic

Index

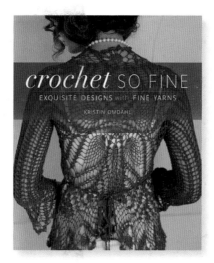
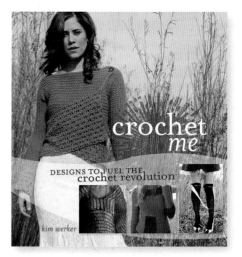